Libya

Libya

BY TERRI WILLIS

Enchantment of the World™
Second Series

Children's Press®

An Imprint of Scholastic Inc.

NEW YORK   TORONTO   LONDON   AUCKLAND   SYDNEY
MEXICO CITY   NEW DELHI   HONG KONG
DANBURY, CONNECTICUT

Frontispiece: The Roman ruins of Leptis Magna, near al-Khums

Consultant: Ogenga Otunnu, Professor of History, DePaul University, Chicago, Illinois

Please note: All statistics are as up-to-date as possible at the time of publication.

Book production by Herman Adler

Library of Congress Cataloging-in-Publication Data

Willis, Terri.
  Libya / by Terri Willis.
    p. cm.—(Enchantment of the world. Second series)
  Includes bibliographical references and index.
  ISBN-13: 978-0-531-12480-2
  ISBN-10: 0-531-12480-0
  1. Libya—Juvenile literature. [1. Libya.] I. Title.
DT215.W55 2008
961.2—dc22   2007052382

Libya

Contents

Cover photo:
Man at Um
Elmaa Lake

Oasis

Tuareg festival

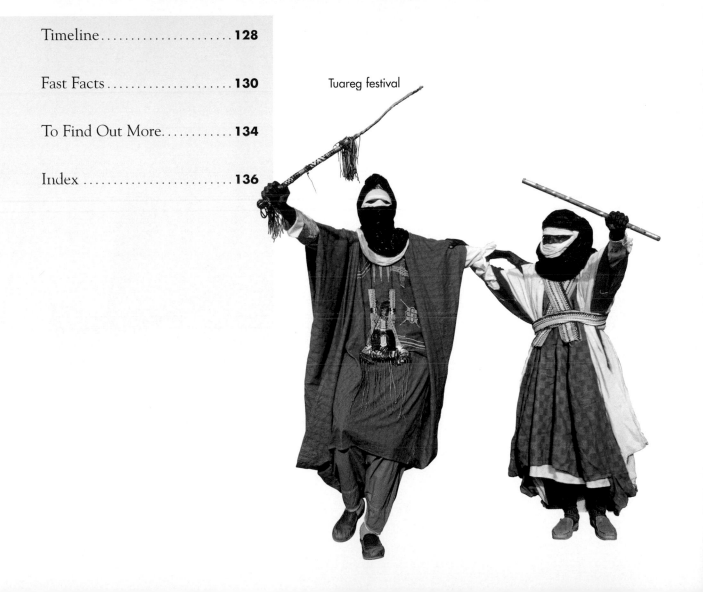

A Framework for Life

Family is the framework of life in Libya. Libyans value their close family and community ties. This tradition dates to the time when most people in Libya were nomads. Wandering the vast desert region known as the Sahara in search of water and grazing land, they had to depend on one another. Though isolated, nomads were sociable. They usually traveled in groups, and they warmly greeted strangers who came upon their campsites. Nomads knew that to turn people

Opposite: **A man plays a flutelike instrument called a *ghita* at Sabratha, near Tripoli.**

Family is central to Libyan life. Here, a man from the Tuareg ethnic group kisses his son.

out on the desert alone would likely cause their death, so instead, they fed strangers and cared for them, traditionally for three days. Libyans today still value visiting family and friends. They're generous, welcoming, and eager to share meals.

Nearly all people in Libya are Muslims, followers of the religion of Islam. Their faith is part of their birth and part of their death, and it fills much of the life that comes between. Prayer is central to the everyday lives of Muslims—Islam requires that they pray five times daily. And the mosque, the Muslim house of worship, is central to each city or village.

A nomad bows in prayer before heading out on his journey. All Muslims, no matter where they are, pray five times a day.

Some aspects of Libyan society have changed in recent decades. For centuries, Libyans were cut off from much of the rest of the world. Nomads didn't receive much news or information from the outside world. They lived as they had for generations. Then, in the middle of the twentieth century, oil was discovered in Libya. This brought money and new possibilities and challenges to the nation. But Libya's leaders kept the nation's citizens isolated, especially from Western ideas.

Libya has the best record of children's health care of any nation in Africa.

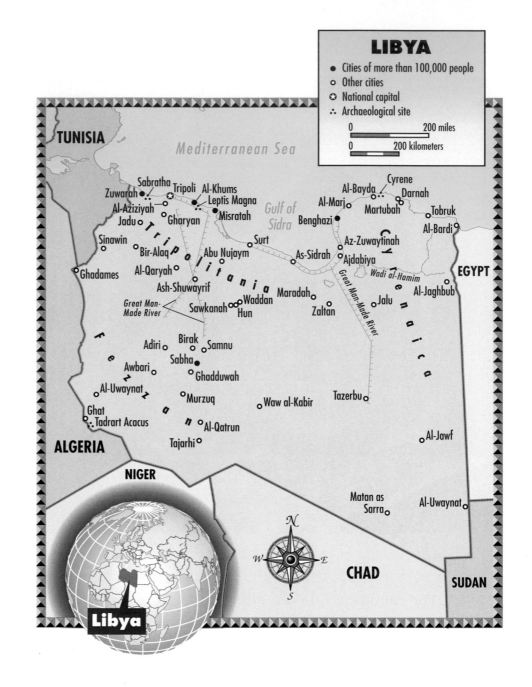

In recent years, though, Libya has begun to open up. The government is working to improve relationships with Western nations, and that's having an influence on Libyan life. Libyan fashion, music, and art continue to evolve. People's lives are changing, too. Regardless of these changes, faith and family will continue to provide the foundation for the lives of the people of Libya.

Some Libyan women wear Western-style clothing. Most also wear a scarf over their hair because they want to dress modestly.

From Sea to Sand

ABOUT 90 PERCENT OF LIBYA IS COVERED WITH DESERT. Much of it is a great swath of swirling sand called the Sahara. But there is more to the desert than sand, and Libya is more than just desert.

Libya's northern border is a beautiful coastline. Its green fields and sun-drenched beaches stretch for about 1,100 miles (1,770 kilometers) along the Mediterranean Sea. High mountains reach toward the sky in the southwest. Algeria and Tunisia lie to the west of Libya. Chad and Niger lie to the south. To the east, Libya shares a border with Egypt and Sudan.

Opposite: **Few trees can survive in the shifting sands of the Sahara.**

Waves on the Mediterranean crash ashore near Tripoli. More than 85 percent of Libyans live near the coast.

Libya's Geographic Features

Area: 679,362 square miles (1,759,540 sq km)

Highest Elevation: Bikku Bitti (Bette Peak), 7,438 feet (2,267 m) above sea level

Lowest Elevation: Sabkhat Ghuzayyil, 154 feet (47 m) below sea level

Coastline: 1,100 miles (1,770 km)

Highest Annual Precipitation: 16 inches (40 cm), near Tripoli

Lowest Annual Precipitation: Less than 1 inch (2.5 cm), in the Sahara

Highest Recorded Temperature: 136°F (58°C), in al-Aziziyah in 1922

Highest Average Temperature: 88°F (31°C), at Sabha in July

Lowest Average Temperature: 47°F (8°C), in Tripoli in January

Greatest Distance North to South: 930 miles (1,500 km)

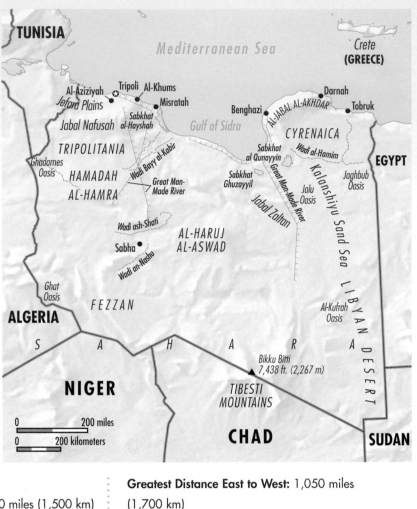

Greatest Distance East to West: 1,050 miles (1,700 km)

With 679,362 square miles (1,759,540 sq km) of land, Libya is Africa's fourth-largest country. Only Algeria, Congo, and Sudan are larger. Libya is slightly larger than the state of Alaska. The nation is divided into three regions—Tripolitania, Fezzan, and Cyrenaica—each with its own distinct character.

Tripolitania

Tripolitania covers northwestern Libya, from the Tunisian border to the Gulf of Sidra and inland for several hundred miles. The city of Tripoli, Libya's capital, sits on the coast in this region. Nearly one-third of Libya's people live in and around Tripoli.

Part of Tripolitania is a swath of low-lying land, about 6 miles (10 km) wide and 185 miles (300 km) long, along the coast of the Mediterranean. Sand flats and marshy lagoons fill this strip of land. Tripolitania also has vast stretches of coarse grass broken up by *wadis*—riverbeds that remain dry except during the rainy season, when they fill with water rushing toward the sea.

Tripoli is a sprawling city that hugs the Mediterranean coast. The city and its suburbs are home to more than 1.5 million people.

The coast is an important agricultural region. Fields of wheat, barley, soybeans, cauliflower, and tomatoes blanket the region. Groves of trees produce dates, almonds, peanuts, olives, and citrus fruits.

Inland from the coast, the land slowly rises to merge with the Jefara Plains. The broad, flat plains stretch scrubby and desert-like until they reach Jabal Nafusah, a series of limestone hills. Old craters and lava rocks indicate that volcanoes created these hills in ancient times. Today, the hills of Jabal Nafusah, which reach heights of about 3,000 feet (900 meters), support little more than a few fig trees.

Traveling southward, the hills gradually taper into the Hamadah al-Hamra, also known as the Red Desert. Its name comes from the red sandstone that underlies it. The Red Desert sweeps across hundreds of miles until it reaches Fezzan.

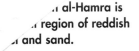

al-Hamra is region of reddish and sand.

Rough rocks rise above the sands in Fezzan.

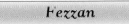

Fezzan

Fezzan is a desert area, and its 212,808 square miles (551,170 sq km) make up most of southwestern Libya. In Fezzan, vast sand dunes—some several hundred feet high—change shape slowly with the shifting wind. These dunes, called *ergs* in Arabic, cover about one-fifth of Fezzan. Much of the rest is jagged, rocky plateau. The wind and the intense temperature changes of the desert carve some of the rocks into odd shapes.

Depressions called *sabkhas* pepper the land in Fezzan. The sabkhas look like large bowls on the desert floor. Many of these depressions contain underground water, which creates oasis areas, or oases.

Desert Oases

An oasis is a patch of green in a sea of sand. Its deep underground wells or springs provide enough water for trees, grass, and shrubs to grow. In some large oases, villages have formed, and people grow crops. As few as one or two families may live in smaller oases.

Oases are the traditional lands of nomads, who wander in search of grazing land for their animals, and fresh supplies of food and water for themselves. These desert nomads, called Bedouin, find most of these resources on the oases. Few Libyans are nomads today. Since the discovery of oil in 1959, most Bedouin have moved to the urban areas of northern Libya.

More than six hundred million years ago, a gigantic mountain range covered Fezzan. As time passed, the sea advanced over the region and then retreated again. Scientists have found evidence of this ancient sea in marine fossils in the desert. Over the centuries, water, wind, and temperature changes worked together to erode the mountains, resulting in the sands and plateaus of today.

Most of Fezzan is fairly flat, but the Tibesti Mountains rise in the south along the border with Chad. These mountains include Bikku Bitti (Bette Peak), the highest point in Libya at 7,438 feet (2,267 m).

Trucks rumble through an area between sand dunes in the Ubari Desert in Fezzan. Vast areas of sand dunes such as the Ubari are sometimes called sand seas.

Cyrenaica

...he northeastern part of Libya, is the country's

...hic region, covering nearly half the land. This

... Libya's eastern Mediterranean coast, another

...cultural area, which supports vineyards and fruit

...ards. Cyrenaica has three important port cities: Benghazi,
Darnah, and Tobruk.

South of the coast, the land rises steeply about 2,900 feet
(880 m) to a rocky plateau called al-Jabal al-Akhdar, or the
Green Mountain. This name probably comes from the flowers

...flat
...e in

...m)
...most of
...ibya.

Al-Jabal al-Akhdar rises near the coast in Cyrenaica.

that cover the mountain's lower slopes, including anemones, cyclamens, lilies, and narcissuses. At higher elevations, scrubby shrubs and juniper grow. The Green Mountain extends south all the way to the Libyan Desert, a part of the Sahara.

Some sections of the Libyan Desert are bare and rocky. Other sections are sandy. With the exception of a few oases, all if it is harsh and inhospitable. Al-Kufrah, one of the largest oases in Libya, lies in this region. It was once an important stop for caravans of traders making their way across the Sahara.

Total Eclipse

Thousands of tourists flocked to Libya in the days before March 29, 2006. They wanted to get a glimpse of an unusual event—a total solar eclipse. A solar eclipse happens when the moon passes between the earth and the sun, blocking the sun's light. A total solar eclipse, when all the light is blocked, is rare. Before 2006, Africa hadn't seen a total solar eclipse in more than twenty-seven years. The darkness, which cut a swath through the Sahara, lasted a little more than four minutes.

During that time, some Muslims recited a special prayer said only during a total solar eclipse. The *Salat al-Kusoo* thanks Allah (which is "God" in Arabic) for the beauty of the eclipse.

...with
...
...
...Greeks
...center of oil
...s and visitors buy
...ed, an outdoor market,
...beaches.

...third-largest city, is located east of
...nwestern Libya. Its population is nearly
...dred thousand. Some of the world's tallest sand dunes separate Misratah from the Mediterranean Sea. The city began in about A.D. 800 as a supply center for caravans and has been a trading center ever since. Today, groves of palm and olive trees surround the town. Mainly non-Libyans work in the two iron and steel mills that form Misratah's main industry. Many craftspeople in Misratah make carpets, baskets, and pottery.

Al-Khums has more than three hundred thousand residents, making it Libya's fourth-largest city. It lies on the northwest coast, about 60 miles (100 km) southeast of Tripoli. Workers in al-Khums process tuna, olive oil, and other foods and manufacture products such as soap and cement. The nearby ancient Roman city of Leptis Magna (left) makes tourism important to al-Khums as well.

Climate

More than 90 percent of Libya is desert, so it should not come as a surprise that the country is hot and dry. Daytime summer temperatures in the Sahara average almost 100 degrees Fahrenheit (38 degrees Celsius) and often reach 115°F (46°C). It's cooler in the winter, with temperatures of only 60 or 70°F (16 or 21°C). And in the high mountain ranges along Libya's southern border, it can get downright cold, with ice and snow on the ground at times.

In the heat of the day, most Libyans try to stay in the shade.

...lls the air in Jabal .Nafusah.

Only a light amount of rain falls in the desert—about 4 inches (10 centimeters) per year, and as little as 0.2 inches (0.5 cm) in some years. In the spring and fall, desert winds build up, carrying swirls of dust and sand all the way north to the Mediterranean Sea. These hot winds, called *ghiblis*, usually last one to four days. They can damage the coastal cereal crops in the spring, but in the fall, their warmth makes the date crop ripen faster.

The Mediterranean Sea affects weather in Libya's coastal areas. Summers are hot and humid. Winters are much cooler, and most of the year's 14 to 22 inches (36 to 56 cm) of rain falls then. Farther south, the plains region of Cyrenaica gets the heaviest rainfall in Libya—about 26 inches (66 cm) yearly. These rains often cause flash floods because the parched ground does not absorb moisture easily.

Date palms and other trees thrive in oases in Sabha.

Water

Libya has no rivers that flow throughout the year. Its only rivers form during the rainy season following heavy downpours. Libya is among the ten countries in the world with the fewest renewable water resources.

Libya borders the Mediterranean Sea, but water for agriculture is in short supply. Seawater can't be used to grow crops because as it evaporates, it leaves salt behind, damaging the soil. Many of the wells that supplied freshwater to Libya's farms for centuries are nearly dry. Others have become too salty to use as seawater seeps into them.

Since 1984, Libyans have been working on an enormous project, the Great Man-Made River, which is tapping into large reserves of freshwater under the desert. The water has been there, trapped between layers of rock and sand, for about thirty thousand years. It slowly filtered down as the glaciers of the last ice age melted. People are now building pipelines to carry the water hundreds of miles north to Libya's farming region.

The first water to flow through the pipeline arrived in Tripoli in 1996. In September 2007, water began flowing to Gharyan, south of Tripoli—the second phase of the project. Much more work remains. According to the plans, more than 3,000 miles (5,000 km) of water pipeline will eventually stretch across the nation.

The Great Man-Made River is controversial. Some geologists caution that draining the water from beneath the ground will weaken the land above and may cause dangerous cave-ins. Most agree that the underground water will be used up within fifty years. Many people believe that the cost for the project has been too high for something that won't last long. But Libyan leader Muammar al-Qaddafi has supported the project since it started. He dismissed the criticism, calling the Great Man-Made River the "eighth wonder of the world."

One Hot Day

The hottest temperature ever officially recorded on the planet was in Libya, in the Sahara. On September 13, 1922, the temperature at al-Aziziyah reached 136°F (58°C) in the shade. Since then, people have unofficially recorded higher temperatures in other parts of the Sahara.

Great Man-Made River Facts

- The total projected cost is US$25 billion.
- The project will eventually include 1,300 wells, which will supply an estimated 1.7 billion gallons (6.4 million cubic meters) of water each day.
- The concrete-reinforcing wire used in the project could circle the earth 280 times.
- More than 70 percent of the water supplied by the Great Man-Made River will go to farms, irrigating approximately 320,000 acres (130,000 hectares) of agricultural land.
- The Great Man-Made River is made of pipes 13 feet (4 m) in diameter, large enough to drive a truck through.

Desert Life

Little rain falls in most of Libya. For trees to survive, they must get water from under the ground.

THE MILD CLIMATE AND FERTILE LANDS OF LIBYA'S coastal region support a variety of plants and animals. But the desert that dominates most of the nation presents a challenge to living things. Plants and animals in Libya must be able to survive in extreme heat and with little water.

Ships of the Desert

The first desert animal people think of is the camel. Camels have sometimes been called "ships of the desert." For centuries, just as people relied on ships as the only means of transport

Opposite: **A camel caravan makes its way across the Sahara.**

Ode to a Camel

Traditionally, the nomads of Libya relied on camels and honored them. When visitors arrived at a Bedouin campsite, the hosts met the camels' needs first, before those of their human guests. Nomads believed that people would be judged after death on the kindness they showed to camels during life. And nomads often praised camels in folk songs and poetry:

My camel is like lightning,
the finest of animals;
When it turns its head towards me
Its hair feels soft as silk.

across oceans, people relied on camels as the only way to travel across deserts. The camel is uniquely suited for the task because it can live for more than a week without water. Camels first arrived in North Africa in the first century A.D., when Persians brought them from Asia to Egypt. Within one hundred years, they became common throughout the region.

A camels can store about 50 gallons (190 l) of water in the three sections of its stomach. After several days without water, a camel can drink an astonishing amount—sometimes 25 gallons (95 l) at one time! The hump on the camel's back is a large lump of fat that will nourish the animal when there is no other food available.

Camels have other features that allow them to thrive in the desert. They can close their eyes and nostrils so tightly during a windstorm that not a speck of sand blows in. They can survive eating nothing but thorny desert shrubs and the pits of dates. The big, wide, leathery soles of their feet keep camels from sinking into the sand and also help them walk across rocky ground. And camels can smell water from as far away as 1 mile (1.6 km)!

For centuries, the lives of Libya's nomads centered on camels. Camels can carry as much as 1,000 pounds (450 kilograms) at a time. People can drink camel milk and make cheese from it. Dried camel droppings make good fuel to burn in campfires. When woven, the soft hair from the bellies of camels makes warm cloth strong enough for making tents.

Nomads stop for tea while their camels look on. Many of Libya's nomads now travel by truck rather than camel.

Today, many nomads have replaced their camels with trucks. People no longer measure wealth by the number of camels a person owns. But camels remain an important part of Libya's history and culture.

Other Desert Mammals

Other animals also do well in the desert. Some adapt to the harsh climate through estivation—staying inactive during the hot summer months. Estivation is somewhat like hibernation, sleeping through the cold winter. Many rodents practice estivation. Some insects and birds such as nighthawks also survive through estivation.

Jerboas are the size of mice and have powerful back legs. Some jerboas can leap 10 feet (3 m) at a time.

Dressing for the Desert

Most mammals in the Libyan Desert, including Barbary sheep (above), have light, sandy-colored fur and skin. This trait helps them in two ways. First, their light coloring blends with the background of sand and rocks, so their enemies have difficulty finding them. Having a body that naturally blends with the landscape is called camouflage. Second, light colors reflect heat from the sun, so their coloring actually helps the desert animals stay cooler.

Other animals, like jerboas, are nocturnal, meaning they sleep during the day and come out at night. The jerboa is a small, mouselike creature that hops like a tiny kangaroo. It balances itself with a 6-inch (15 cm) tail that is nearly as long as its body. The jerboa stays under the sand during the scorching heat of the day. It comes out at night when it is cooler to feed on desert plants and insects. Like some other desert animals, the jerboa does not drink any water at all. It gets all the water it needs from the food it eats.

The fennec fox's large ears give it excellent hearing. It can hear the movement of distant prey, even if the prey is underground in a burrow.

Some desert animals, such as fennec foxes, hyenas, and wildcats, are carnivores, or meat eaters. They constantly roam the desert hunting for prey. Fennecs get all the water they need to survive by eating other desert animals and insects—especially jerboas. Fennecs have huge ears, which help keep them cool. The heat escapes their bodies through their ears.

In the past, many desert gazelles lived in Libya. Like fennecs and jerboas, gazelles are so well adapted to living in the desert that they can go long periods without drinking any liquids. They get all the moisture they need from the plants they eat, which are mostly leaves and flowers. If they find water, they'll drink it, but they don't need it. Desert gazelles are rarely seen today because hunters have killed so many.

The addax antelope still lives near the Algerian border, where it grazes on coarse grass and tough bushes. The addax can weigh up to 265 pounds (120 kg) and travels easily over the sand on its wide hooves.

Insects, Reptiles, and More

Many small desert creatures are most active during the night. When the sun goes down, spiders, centipedes, and poisonous scorpions roam the desert floor, along with grasshoppers and beetles. Some spiders keep the heat out of their homes by plugging their holes with sand.

Sixteen species of venomous scorpions live in Libya. Four of them can be deadly to humans.

Several types of lizards and poisonous snakes live in Libya's deserts. Reptiles are cold-blooded, meaning their temperature changes with their surroundings. At night, their bodies become chilled, so in the morning they lie in the sun to get warm before sneaking back under the sand. A common lizard in Libya is the skink. It uses its wedge-shaped jaw to dig holes in the sand where it hides and cools off. Its eyes are covered with transparent scales that prevent irritation from the sand.

Snakes in Libya include the horned viper, Cleopatra's asp, and several types of adder. Brightly colored kraits stand out against the dull sand and rocks during the light of day, so they hunt at night when they can easily sink their grooved fangs into unsuspecting victims.

Desert birds include vultures and hawks. The sand grouse is well suited for life in a dry climate. Its water-absorbing feathers allow the adult birds to carry moisture back to their nests to cool their eggs.

Horned vipers blend in well with the rocky desert. They get their name from the small horns above each eye.

Hardy acacia trees have long roots that allow them to tap the groundwater deep beneath the desert.

Oasis Creatures

A wider variety of animals live in the oases than in the deserts. Oases give shelter to many mice and rats as well as bats and several types of birds, including warblers, larks, grouses, desert bullfinches, and turtledoves. Butterflies and dragonflies dart through the air and sometimes venture into the desert.

Plant Life

Just as animals in desert regions must adapt to the environment, so too must plants. They must be able to survive the hot, dry conditions. Often, they must grow in salty land. Typically, desert plants have long root systems that tap into groundwater far below the surface. Most have small leaves from which little moisture evaporates.

Date palms grow in an oasis in the Sahara. Some date palms reach heights of 100 feet (30 m).

Plants found in the Sahara are similar to desert plants elsewhere. But the Sahara has a smaller variety of plants than most other deserts. Scrubby grasses are found here and there, but few trees grow outside of the oases.

Date palm trees grow wild in oases and other nonarid parts of Libya. They are hardy trees, thriving even under the extreme heat of summer and chilling frost of winter. Date palm trees are useful in many ways—dates are a delicious fruit, fresh or dried. Date seeds can be ground and mixed with flour, and their sweet juice makes a treat similar to honey. The palm tree trunks are used for lumber and fuel. And the palm fronds are woven into sandals, baskets, and mats. People find ways to use every part of the date palm.

Cactuses are also common in Libyan oases. Many Libyans enjoy eating the sweet, juicy fruit of the prickly pear cactus. Wild pistachios are another treat. Grass grows in most non-desert areas of Libya. Esparto grass, which people use to make paper and rope, was at one time Libya's chief export. Leaves from the henna plant are used to make red dye. Many Libyan women dye their hair with henna, and some use it to paint intricate designs on their hands.

The Lush Desert

In the rare times when heavy rains fall in the Sahara—which usually happens less than once in ten years—the desert blossoms. Grasses, herbs, and flowers spring up. The seeds and bulbs that produce the greenery can survive long, hot, dry periods and still grow into plants.

Young Nation, Ancient Land

Libya as a nation is quite young. It did not become independent until 1951. Still, Libya is an ancient land. Its people have a history rich with stories of kingdoms and wars and overcoming difficulties.

Opposite: **The Garamantes people controlled Fezzan more than two thousand years ago. Their tombs survive to this day.**

Ancient Artists

More than ten thousand years ago, people drew pictures on rocks in each of Libya's three regions. They depicted an environment very different from today's Libya. The artists drew landscapes full of plants—grasses, shrubs, and many kinds of trees, including evergreens. Their drawings showed large herds of animals living near lakes and flowing rivers. Crocodiles, hippopotamuses, zebras, ostriches, and even elephants and giraffes appear in the pictures.

The ancient artists were drawing the world around them—fossil remains of plants and animals found in the area prove it. Between about 10,500 years ago and

Thousands of ancient paintings and carvings grace Tadrart Acacus, a mountainous area in southwestern Libya.

Independent Fezzan

Conquering nations showed less interest in Fezzan than in Tripolitania and Cyrenaica because its desert land was less valuable. The Garamantes ruled Fezzan from about 1000 B.C. to A.D. 500. They controlled much of the trade route across the Sahara along which caravans brought ivory and gold from deep in Africa north to the Mediterranean. Pyramid tombs built by the Garamantes still stand today.

about 6,000 years ago, Libya was covered with jungles, not deserts. When the climate changed and the rivers and plants disappeared, the animals moved south, out of North Africa.

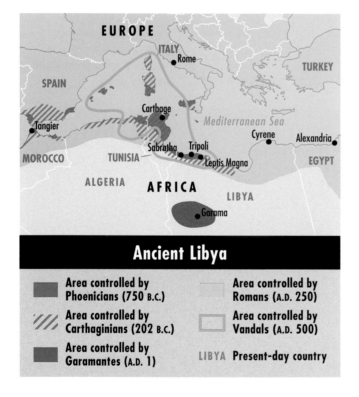

Ancient Libya

Area controlled by Phoenicians (750 B.C.)

Area controlled by Carthaginians (202 B.C.)

Area controlled by Garamantes (A.D. 1)

Area controlled by Romans (A.D. 250)

Area controlled by Vandals (A.D. 500)

LIBYA Present-day country

Early Farmers

Early humans found all the food they needed by hunting and gathering. By around 5000 B.C., people had learned to grow plants and raise cattle. Farming let them live in one place all year. These early settlers of Libya are called the Berbers. Their fertile land was valuable. Outsiders fought to control the Mediterranean coast in the regions of Tripolitania and Cyrenaica.

Outsiders in Charge

Phoenician sailors, from the area that is now Lebanon, established ports on Libya's Mediterranean coast in Tripolitania beginning in 1300 B.C. They wanted places along their trade route from

Phoenicians made ships from cedar trees. They sailed the Mediterranean in their ships, becoming great traders.

Phoenicia to Spain where they could anchor ships. Though they reigned for the next five hundred years, the Phoenicians did little to colonize the region. They did not travel farther inland to establish new communities or to search for resources. Instead, the small Phoenician settlements along Libya's coast depended on their homeland for supplies.

The Phoenicians founded the city of Carthage farther west along the North African coast, in today's Tunisia. Carthage grew into a wealthy seaport and became an independent power in its own right. The city built up a strong military force, and soon Carthaginians ruled much of the Mediterranean's North African coast, including Tripolitania.

Unlike the Phoenicians, the Carthaginians established several colonies, which they ruled harshly. They forced some of the strongest Libyan men to fight for them, while they put the rest of the citizens to work farming. The Carthaginian rulers demanded as much as half of the Libyans' crops each season.

Roman and Carthaginian ships clash in 256 B.C. After battling on and off for more than a hundred years, Rome defeated Carthage in 146 B.C.

Few settlements the Carthaginians built remain today. The most prosperous cities of the time were stopping points in the trade route across the Sahara, linking the Mediterranean Sea with the Niger River, which cuts across western Africa. Along that route, dealers exchanged slaves as well as gemstones, fine cloth, foods, and other goods. Over time, wars and a lack of resources caused the trade route to fade, and the Carthaginian cities faded with it.

Leaving a Mark

The next groups to rule Libya, the Romans and the Greeks, built great cities and monuments, some of which remain standing today. In 146 B.C., Romans took over the Carthaginian Empire. Tripolitania's coastal region became one of the main sources of grain and other foods for the Roman Empire.

The Greek stronghold was in Cyrenaica. Greek explorers and warriors had been visiting the region for hundreds of years. First, they tried to use the region as a route to invade

Egypt. Later, Cyrenaica became a bountiful Greek fishing area. When the Greeks realized that Cyrenaica was the only part of North Africa that no one had colonized, they took greater control of the land. At first the region prospered, but as more Greeks moved in to share the wealth, the local people began to rebel, sometimes successfully. Control of the land changed hands many times. Eventually Cyrenaica, too, fell under Roman rule.

The area continued to prosper for several hundred years, and the population grew. Libya's largest city at the time was Leptis Magna, which had about eighty thousand citizens in A.D. 200. But as their empire began to buckle, the Romans lost control of North Africa.

The Marble Arch

An ancient white marble arch stands in Tripoli, Libya's largest city and capital. The Romans built the arch in about A.D. 163 to honor Marcus Aurelius, who had become emperor of Rome a few years earlier. At the time, the Roman Empire seemed to be in decline. Invading groups threatened the empire, and all but the top members of the upper class suffered from poverty. Marcus restored much of the empire's glory. He passed laws to improve the lives of enslaved workers, and he made sure that the Roman Empire had a strong military to protect it from invaders.

Preserving History

The United Nations Educational, Scientific, and Cultural Organization (UNESCO) chooses cultural and natural sites around the world for preservation. UNESCO says these places, called World Heritage sites, have unusual importance to humanity. Libya has five World Heritage sites.

Cyrene is the remains of an ancient Greek colony. One structure on the site began as a Greek shrine. The Romans enlarged it and turned it into an amphitheater where trained fighters called gladiators battled wild animals. Other monuments at Cyrene include the Temple of Apollo and the Sanctuary of Zeus.

Leptis Magna (below) was one of the grandest cities in the Roman world, with a beautiful harbor and ornate marble and granite buildings. After suffering several attacks, the city fell into ruins. It was abandoned in

the 600s, and sand quickly buried it. Leptis Magna was not uncovered until the early twentieth century. Today, the ruins of houses, a market, a church, and other buildings have been uncovered. Some of the monuments have been moved to museums, while others have been restored on the site, which is about 75 miles (120 km) east of Tripoli.

Sabratha (above) was a flourishing Phoenician port city during the second and third centuries A.D. The site includes a beautiful theater surrounded on three sides by pink and white marble walls.

Tadrart Acacus is located in southwestern Libya, east of the city of Ghat. Cave paintings here, some twelve thousand years old, show how differently plants, animals, and human life appeared then. Some visitors and photographers have damaged the site by wetting the drawings to make them stand out better.

Ghadames is a tranquil oasis settlement. People have lived on the site for at least five thousand years. Inside its walled city are clusters of homes made of clay and brick. Most have several floors. Traditionally, people used the ground floor for storage, while family life took place on upper floors. The open terraces on the roofs were the realm of women.

The next group to sweep into Libya were the Vandals, who came from the part of Europe that is now Germany. Attracted by North Africa's wealth, they arrived in the region in about A.D. 435. Among the invaders, the Vandals made the first serious attempts to settle some of Libya's mountain and desert areas. But the nomadic people who lived in these regions often rebelled. The Vandals lost power after about a century of rule. Soon a new group took over, and they would have a much greater effect on the region.

Arabs in Libya

When the Arabs arrived in 643, they brought the new religion of Islam with them. The people in the region quickly adopted Islam. Within four hundred years, most people in Libya were Muslims.

Today, 97 percent of Libyans are Muslim, and the Arabic language is dominant throughout the country. Most Libyans today claim Arab heritage. No other invaders played such a large role in shaping present-day Libya.

Although the Arabs had the most lasting effect, other invaders continued to arrive on Libya's shores. Normans from Europe captured Tripoli in 1146, and then a Muslim army from Morocco took control of the city in 1158. Called the Almohads, these

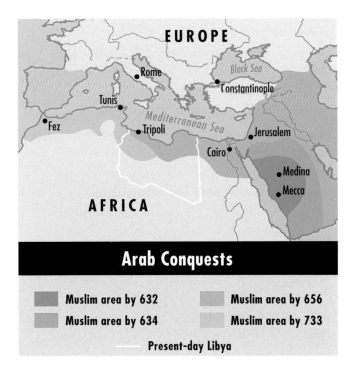

Arab Conquests

Muslim area by 632   Muslim area by 656

Muslim area by 634   Muslim area by 733

—— Present-day Libya

invaders extended their reign over most of Tripolitania during the next two hundred years. In 1510, Spain captured Tripoli. The Spanish controlled the city until 1551, when Ottoman Turks took over Tripoli and, eventually, all of Libya. The Ottoman Empire had its base in Turkey and spread over southeastern Europe, the Middle East, and North Africa.

Like all the other groups that had invaded Libya, the Ottomans faced the opposition of the Libyan people. The Libyans were proud and did not easily accept foreign rule. Throughout history, groups of Libyan rebels often tried to resist the invaders. Many of the resistance leaders had ties to a religious organization called the Sanusi Brotherhood.

The Sanusi Brotherhood

The Sanusi Brotherhood was a religious group that played a major role in Libya's political history. The brotherhood was established in 1837 by Sidi Muhammad ibn-Ali al-Sanusi to promote a return to the simple beliefs and lifestyle of early Islam. It was also a missionary order aimed at spreading Islam throughout the region.

The brotherhood's leader was known as the Grand Sanusi. Members pledged him their allegiance, both religious and political. The brotherhood established lodges, called *zawiyas*, throughout Cyrenaica and in parts of Tripolitania. The zawiyas became influential, providing political and spiritual guidance to members. The zawiyas were at the center of resistance movements against several invaders, including the French during the Ottoman period, and the Italians.

Later, Sanusi leaders represented the Libyan people in negotiations with the Italians and with the British after World War II. Libya's only king, Idris I (below), who ruled from 1951 to 1969, was the Grand Sanusi when he was made king.

Barbary Pirates

In the late 1700s, Barbary pirates, named for the Berbers, controlled parts of the Mediterranean. They sailed out of Tripoli to raid ships, including American merchant ships. The pirates stole goods and kidnapped crew members as slaves and sometimes held them for ransom. At one point, Barbary pirates held nearly twenty-five thousand captives for ransom. The pirates also demanded money, called tribute, from nations in return for allowing their ships to travel through the Mediterranean without harassment.

Beginning in 1795, the United States paid the pirate leaders a yearly tribute of more than US$2 million. In 1801, when the pirate leaders demanded even higher payments, the United States refused and fighting broke out. The United States created its navy to battle these pirates. The "Marines' Hymn," the official song of the U.S. Marine Corps, refers to this origin of the U.S. Navy in its opening line: "From the halls of Montezuma to the shores of Tripoli."

The U.S. Navy defeated the Barbary pirates at Tripoli in 1805. The pirates agreed to lower the tribute costs, and the United States continued to pay until 1815. After that, skirmishes began anew and lasted for several years until the pirates' power dwindled.

The Italian Invasion

The Ottoman Empire ruled Libyan territory for more than three centuries before its control began to weaken. As the Ottomans lost their grip on Libya, the Italians moved in. Italy wanted to colonize Libya for several reasons. Control of Tripoli would give Italy greater shipping power in the Mediterranean Sea. Italy also wanted a presence in North Africa. The British already controlled Egypt, and the Italians feared that France wanted Libya. After months of fighting against the invading

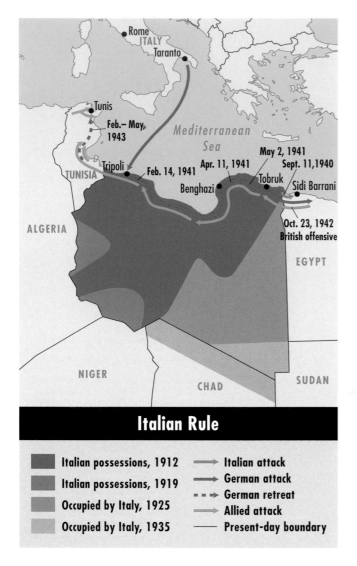

Italian Rule

- Italian possessions, 1912
- Italian possessions, 1919
- Occupied by Italy, 1925
- Occupied by Italy, 1935
- → Italian attack
- → German attack
- ---→ German retreat
- → Allied attack
- — Present-day boundary

Map labels: Rome, ITALY, Taranto, Tunis, Feb.–May, 1943, Mediterranean Sea, Tripoli, TUNISIA, Feb. 14, 1941, Apr. 11, 1941, May 2, 1941, Sept. 11,1940, Benghazi, Tobruk, Sidi Barrani, ALGERIA, Oct. 23, 1942 British offensive, EGYPT, NIGER, CHAD, SUDAN

Italian forces, the Ottomans finally gave up their rights to Libya in 1911.

When the Italians discovered the remains of cities built by their Roman ancestors centuries before, they declared that Libya was rightfully theirs. Soon, thousands of Italians moved to Libya, and the Italian military made ferocious attempts to wipe out the Arabs. Death was the punishment for those who resisted. Many whom the Italians didn't kill were confined in concentration camps. Italians cemented over community wells in several Arab settlements, forcing the people to either scatter in search of water or die. They also killed herds of cattle.

The few positive changes under Italian rule were mostly intended to help the Italian settlers. The Italians improved roads and ports and built new irrigation systems to deliver water to dry desert lands. They brought in farm machinery to help produce more crops.

Libyans hated Italian rule. A teacher named Omar al-Mukhtar organized a few hundred men in the city of Barga and in the Green Mountain region, in northeast Libya. Their group was called the *Mujahedeen,* or "Freedom Fighters." With good horses but old military equipment, the resistance battled tens of thousands of Italian troops. The Libyans showed early success at holding back the Italian invaders, and their numbers grew to several thousand men and women. Aided by the Turks, the Libyan resistance army almost defeated the Italians during World War I (1914–1918).

Freedom Fighter

Omar al-Mukhtar (1862–1931) was a teacher and Qur'an scholar who loved his studies, but he became a man of action when he could no longer tolerate Italian rule. He pulled together the Mujahedeen, a resistance movement that nearly forced the Italians from Libya.

Al-Mukhtar became known as the Mentor of Bravery for his fearless leadership of the Mujahedeen. He skillfully tracked the movements of the Italians and used his great knowledge of the Libyan landscape to ambush them.

By the time he was eighty years old, al-Mukhtar had led the Mujahedeen for nearly twenty years. In 1931, he was wounded in battle and captured. The Italians shackled him in heavy chains. They tried and convicted him, and then they hanged him on September 16, 1931, in front of thousands of mourning Libyans. Today, al-Mukhtar is honored as one of Libya's greatest heroes.

Libya was not finally freed from Italian rule until 1943, when Italy was defeated in World War II. After the war, the United Nations (UN), an international organization established to foster peace, decided that Libya should become a constitutional monarchy. Under this system of government, a king or queen rules, but with limited powers.

After centuries of foreign rule, Libya became an independent nation in 1951, officially called the Kingdom of Libya. The national assembly chose Libya's first king, Muhammad Idris al-Sanusi, who had been a leader of the Libyan resistance movement against Italy. The king appointed a governor for each of the three regional provinces that together made up Libya.

The Italians were defeated in North Africa in 1943. Here, Italian troops surrender to Allied forces in Libya.

Muhammad Idris al-Sanusi addresses a crowd from a balcony in Tripoli a few months before he was declared king. Idris was the grandson of Sidi Muhammad ibn-Ali al-Sanusi, the founder of the Sanusi Brotherhood.

A Struggling Nation

The new nation had many problems. Each of the three provinces was used to working in its own best interests, so they cooperated little. Also, poverty racked the country. Most people made their living by farming, selling a few small items in villages, or hunting and gathering what they could as they wandered across the desert. In 1951, Libya was one of the most economically underdeveloped nations in the world.

King Idris forced the leader of the opposition out of the country. Though he made improvements in the nation's health and education systems, the lives of ordinary Libyan people didn't get much better. Those among the king's favored group of people did get rich, however.

The oil company Esso made the first big oil strike in Libya in 1959. The company quickly built pipelines and refineries and began shipping oil out of the country in 1961.

Striking Oil

In June 1959, the joyful cheers of workers in the Libyan Desert signaled change. They had struck oil! Libya was on its way to becoming a major world economic force.

The oil strike came at a good time. As people around the world drove more and more cars, they needed more oil to fuel them. As the price of oil rose, Libya profited. Jobs were created. The country strengthened its military force. Schools, health care, roads, communications, housing—oil supplied money to improve all of these.

Still, most of the oil money stayed in the hands of the select few. Most Libyans lived the same impoverished lives they had before the discovery of oil. Though more goods and services became available, the cost of living went up, too.

Qaddafi in Charge

By the late 1960s, King Idris was growing old, and his government was growing increasingly corrupt. Many Libyans complained that he allowed too many Western ideas to influence Libya. In 1969, while the king was out of the country for medical treatment, a rebel military group seized the palace, took over the nation's military bases, and locked up the king's supporters. Muammar al-Qaddafi, the leader of the rebel group, then announced on the radio to the people of Libya that he

Gaddafi or Qadhdhafi?

How do you spell the name of the leader of Libya? There is no one answer. In English, you might spell it Qaddafi, Gaddafi, Gadhafi, or Qadhdhafi. This is because there is no standard system for converting the letters of the Arabic alphabet to the Latin alphabet, which is used to write English and other Western languages. As a result, the spelling of Arabic names in English-language publications varies. If you search on the Internet, you can find more than thirty possible spellings for the Libyan leader's name.

had overthrown the government. Qaddafi, only twenty-seven years old, was the new leader of Libya.

Once Qaddafi took power, changes happened quickly. He renamed the country the Libyan Arab Republic and shut down all the agencies of the old government. Eventually, Qaddafi reorganized Libya's government to include more people, but he continued to hold most of the power.

The streets of Tripoli were deserted in the days after Qaddafi took over Libya.

Qaddafi's Boyhood Training

Muammar al-Qaddafi is a Bedouin. He grew up as part of a nomadic ethnic group that raised small herds of goats and camels and moved frequently in search of food and water. They lived in homes made of goatskin stretched across sticks embedded in the sand. Because they rarely settled, nomads seldom became leaders outside of their own group. Few national leaders come from nomadic backgrounds.

But Qaddafi stood apart even at an early age. He was a bright student and eagerly absorbed Muslim teachings. He loved the traditions of prayer and religious study. His family recognized his abilities and sent their ten-year-old son to an Islamic boarding school in the coastal city of Surt.

Most of Qaddafi's classmates came from wealthy families who lived in cities along Libya's coast. Their fathers were businessmen who had made money dealing with Europeans and Americans after World War II. Western traditions and values greatly influenced most of these families. They were Muslim but had left many traditional beliefs behind.

Qaddafi was different, and not only because he was economically disadvantaged. Several of his relatives had died fighting the Italians and other foreigners who had tried to control Libya. Qaddafi had no use for the Western traditions—the food, clothing, and entertainment—that his classmates so enjoyed. He became a loner and immersed himself in his schoolwork, quickly rising to the top of his class.

To fill his lonely hours, he listened to Egyptian radio programs that featured speeches by Gamal Abdel Nasser, who was then president of Egypt. Nasser often spoke of his desire for political cooperation among Arab nations. He wanted Arab nations to reject Western ties. Young Qaddafi heartily embraced this philosophy.

Qaddafi eventually transferred to a new school, in Sabha. This school included more children of other economically disadvantaged families. They were eager to hear Qaddafi's ideas. Qaddafi was serious and energetic. He soon gathered a large but secretive group around him. They were already plotting the eventual overthrow of King Idris. These plans continued to grow and evolve as Qaddafi went on to the University of Libya and the Libyan Military College and then joined the Libyan Army. In 1969, they came to fruition when twenty-seven-year-old Qaddafi led a rebel group that stormed the king's palace and took control of the country.

Qaddafi also changed Libya's economic system to socialism. He wanted to distribute wealth and property equally among people. The government took control of most property and businesses, though it allowed some people to own small shops.

Part of Qaddafi's plans called for the end of workers earning wages from an employer. Instead, workers would become associates, taking home equal portions of the profits. Workers would also share in the leadership of stores and factories. Unfortunately, sometimes business decisions went unmade. The system bogged down, and the economy came to a standstill. Qaddafi's goal was to end private wealth—he wanted to spread prosperity among all people. But there really wasn't much wealth to spread.

According to reports, many of Libya's wealthiest and best-educated citizens disliked Qaddafi's policies. By the early 1980s, an estimated fifty thousand to one hundred thousand Libyans had fled the country because of the poor economy. These included many of Libya's top technical and business minds.

Troubled Relations

Qaddafi wanted to unite the Arab world, with Libya as a major power. He met with leaders of many Arab nations, but most plans eventually fell through. Many Arab leaders found Qaddafi too aggressive to deal with. Libya also had poor relations with most of its neighboring countries. It fought a border war with Chad for more than twenty years and had tense relations with other North African and Arab nations, including Egypt, Morocco, Sudan, Tunisia, and Syria.

Qaddafi met with South African leader Nelson Mandela in 1997. Qaddafi's house, which was bombed by U.S. forces, is visible in the background.

Libya's relations with the Western world, especially the United States, soured as well. Many in the West believed that Qaddafi wanted to destroy the Jewish state of Israel. In its place, he wanted a nation for Palestinians.

Throughout the 1980s and 1990s, Western leaders agreed that Qaddafi supported terrorism to achieve his goals. Qaddafi denied this. Some accused Libya of helping arm violent groups in Egypt and Sudan and of giving money to terrorists from other nations. The United States accused Libyans of bombing a site in Berlin, Germany, popular with members of the U.S. military, and of shooting down a French plane over Africa. Libya was accused of aiding attacks on airports in Rome, Italy, and Vienna, Austria.

The United States wanted to send a strong message to Libya that terrorism was unacceptable. So, in 1982, the United States restricted some trade between the two countries by placing sanctions on Libya. They were meant to hurt Libya's economy, especially its oil industry.

Relations between the United States and Libya were sometimes violent. In 1981, Libyan and U.S. Air Force planes exchanged fire over the Mediterranean Sea. Two Libyan planes were shot down. In 1986, the United States bombed what it said were terrorist training sites in Tripoli and Benghazi. Qaddafi's home was in one of the areas bombed. The attack killed dozens of Libyan civilians and soldiers including, according to some reports, Qaddafi's infant daughter. Two of Qaddafi's sons were injured.

Pan American Flight 103

On December 21, 1988, Pan American flight 103 left Frankfurt, Germany, for New York carrying 259 people. The plane blew up

A police officer walks past the wreckage of Pan Am flight 103 in Lockerbie in southern Scotland.

over Lockerbie, Scotland, killing everyone on board and 11 people on the ground. Investigators worked for more than two years to uncover the cause of the explosion. Finally, they found a computer chip among the rubble that linked the crash to two Libyan intelligence officers. In November 1991, a U.S. court charged the two Libyans with planting a bomb that brought down the plane.

Libyan officials denied responsibility for the bombing and refused to turn over the two suspects to the United States or Great Britain, arguing that the men could never get a fair trial in either country. To pressure Qaddafi to change his mind, in 1992 the UN imposed sanctions on Libya. It banned air travel to and from Libya, stopped the sale of military weapons to Libya, and limited the sale of equipment needed by Libya's oil industry. These were in addition to the U.S. sanctions already in place.

For several years, the sanctions seemed to have little effect on Qaddafi. Most economic experts agree that the sanctions mainly hurt ordinary Libyans. They weren't able to get up-to-date medicines and could not fly elsewhere if they needed treatment unavailable in their own country.

Finally, in April 1999, Libya turned over the two Lockerbie bombing suspects on the condition that their trial take place on neutral ground. The trial began in May 2000 in the Netherlands. One suspect was cleared of murder charges, while the other was sentenced to twenty-seven years in prison. In 2003, Libya paid money to the families of those killed in the Lockerbie bombing.

In recent years, Qaddafi has tried to improve relations with other nations. In 2003, he visited the North African nation of Tunisia.

Changes in Libya

In the mid-1990s, Qaddafi had begun forging closer ties with other African nations. He promoted the creation of the African Union, an organization of African nations. The African Union is attempting to foster peace and economic development through political and economic integration of all the nations in Africa.

When Qaddafi agreed to hand over the Lockerbie bombing suspects, it marked a change in how Libya got along with Western nations. Qaddafi began trying to repair Libya's reputation. He wanted Libya to rejoin the international community.

Then, in 2003, the United States invaded Iraq, claiming that Iraq had weapons of mass destruction—nuclear, chemical, or biological weapons (such weapons were never found). After the invasion, Qaddafi announced that his country had weapons of mass destruction but was getting rid of them.

The Amazonian Guard

Qaddafi's personal bodyguards are a group of female martial arts experts called the Amazonian Guard. They were so heavily armed when they traveled to Nigeria with Qaddafi in 2006 that Nigerian security officials wouldn't let them enter the country. Qaddafi was angry and threatened to go back home. Finally, the Nigerians agreed that the Libyans could bring eight pistols into the country.

What caused the changes in Libya? One reason was that oil prices dropped in the 1990s. Libya was suddenly not making as much money from oil, so the sanctions hurt more. Some people suggest that the U.S. invasion of Iraq proved that the United States would act aggressively in the Middle East. Still others say that Qaddafi changed his ways when he realized that his initial plans for Arab unity and revolution would never come to pass. He realized that Libya would be isolated unless it cooperated with Western nations.

In return for Qaddafi's changes, the UN dropped its sanctions in 2003. The following year, the United States lifted most of its trade sanctions against Libya, and Prime Minister Tony Blair of Great Britain became the first Western leader to visit Libya in decades. In 2006, the United States removed Libya from its list of nations that support terrorism.

In 2007, Qaddafi visited French president Nicolas Sarkozy to discuss business deals between the two nations. Qaddafi's visit sparked protests by French people who felt that their nation shouldn't host a dictator who had supported terrorism. Qaddafi countered, "Libya has never committed a terrorist act." Though eager to improve relations with the international community, Qaddafi was in no mood to apologize for past problems. Yes, Libya had paid money to the families of victims of terrorist attacks, but Qaddafi said that his nation could not be held responsible for the actions of a few of its citizens. That was all in the past.

"This struggle, this confrontation is now over," Qaddafi said as 2007 came to an end. "We are into another phase." His country, he added, is "determined to participate in a new world of peace, liberty, and cooperation among nations and civilizations."

British prime minister Tony Blair visited Qaddafi in Libya in 2007. He was the first British prime minister to travel to Libya since 1943.

A Government in Transition

UAMMAR AL-QADDAFI TOOK OVER THE LIBYAN government in 1969 and remained in charge into the twenty-first century. According to Qaddafi, Libya's government is based on three ideals: economic and political freedom for Libyans; unity throughout Libya and the Arab world; and Islamic law as the guide for justice. Qaddafi wrote *The Green Book* to explain his political philosophy. In 1977, Qaddafi gave his nation a new name: The Great Socialist People's Libyan Arab Jamahiriya. Qaddafi coined the term *jamahiriya*, meaning "a republic of the masses"—a place where the people rule and everyone has a voice.

Though Qaddafi has no official title, he is known as the revolutionary leader. The leader is supported by the five-member General Secretariat and the sixteen-member General People's Committee. The secretary of the General People's Committee is the official head of the government.

The Libyan Flag

The Libyan flag displays Qaddafi's total loyalty to Islam. The flag is a simple field of green, the color of Islam. There are no other symbols or decorations on it. It is the only national flag in the world that is just one color.

Government of the People

Qaddafi and his team set up a complex process in which citizens can voice their opinions through local government bodies. Libya is made up of thirty-four municipalities, each divided into zones. The citizens in each zone have their own Basic People's Congress and People's Committees. There are hundreds of these groups throughout Libya. They are supposed to be the backbone of the country, giving everyone a chance to make a difference. They elect people to the 760-member

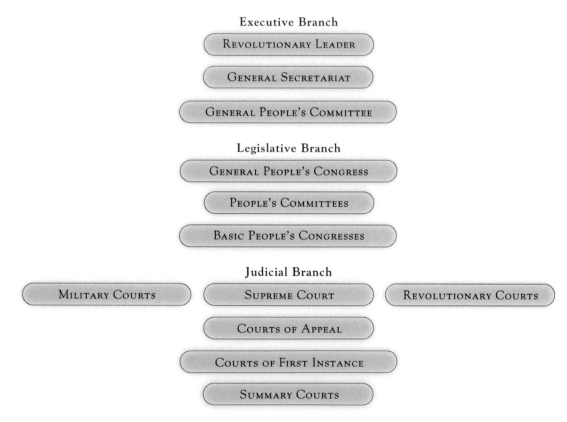

NATIONAL GOVERNMENT OF LIBYA

Executive Branch
- REVOLUTIONARY LEADER
- GENERAL SECRETARIAT
- GENERAL PEOPLE'S COMMITTEE

Legislative Branch
- GENERAL PEOPLE'S CONGRESS
- PEOPLE'S COMMITTEES
- BASIC PEOPLE'S CONGRESSES

Judicial Branch
- MILITARY COURTS
- SUPREME COURT
- REVOLUTIONARY COURTS
- COURTS OF APPEAL
- COURTS OF FIRST INSTANCE
- SUMMARY COURTS

General People's Congress, which considers laws and then sends them to Qaddafi for approval.

Qaddafi waves during a session of the General People's Congress celebrating the anniversary of the revolution.

Who's Really in Charge?

Libya's government structure looks democratic on paper, but the reality is somewhat complex. Although average Libyans have a voice in the Basic People's Congresses and People's Committees, Qaddafi retains central power. He rules with help from the Revolutionary Command Council, his close associates since he took over Libya. They have support from a military ready to defeat any challengers.

Judges on the Libyan Supreme Court listen to testimony in 2007. The General People's Congress appoints the Supreme Court judges.

Libya's Judicial System

Libya's legal system is closely tied to Islam. The nation's constitution is the Qur'an, the holy book of Islam. Laws are shaped by *shari'a*, Islam's religious laws. Drinking alcohol and gambling are forbidden.

Libya's judicial system has four layers. At the bottom are summary courts, located in small towns. People charged with petty offenses such as theft have trials in summary courts. Courts of first instance try more serious crimes.

Those who disagree with the rulings of these two lower courts can take their cases to a court of appeals, where they can argue for a new ruling. Panels of three judges make the final decision. The Supreme Court is Libya's highest court, the final court of appeal. Supreme Court decisions are made by groups of five judges.

Libya also has military courts and revolutionary courts, which aren't part of the regular court system. People charged with committing political offenses and crimes against the state are tried in these courts.

The Military

About twenty-two thousand people serve in Libya's air force, another thirty-five thousand are in the army, and about eight thousand are in the navy. Most members of the Libyan military join because they want to. But Libyan law states that defending the country is the responsibility of all citizens. Men

The HIV Trial

In the late 1990s, 426 Libyan children at a Benghazi children's hospital were infected with HIV, the virus that produces the deadly disease AIDS. The run-down hospital had poor sanitary conditions. In fact, reusing needles probably caused the infection's spread. However, to satisfy the children's grieving families, Libyan authorities accused five Bulgarian nurses and a Palestinian doctor

(the doctor and four of the nurses are shown below) who had worked at the hospital of intentionally infecting the children. Libyan officials claimed that the nurses and the doctor were trying to weaken Qaddafi's authority.

The medical workers were tortured until they confessed. They spent several years in custody before Libyan authorities brought them to trial. Finally, in 2004, they were found guilty and sentenced to death. A second trial in 2006 ended with the same result. Human rights organizations around the world protested the verdicts. On July 17, 2007, the sentences were reduced to life in prison. International organizations continued to pressure Libya, and a week later all of the medical workers were released.

Libya has a shortage of doctors, so its health care system relies on foreign medical workers. If the HIV trial had ended differently, fewer foreign medical workers might have been willing to work in Libya for fear that they, too, might be unjustly accused. Libya's already weak health care system would have weakened further.

and women between the ages of eighteen and thirty-five may be called up for military service at any time. Beginning at age fourteen, Libyan children receive some military training at school. Children ages fifteen through eighteen get weapons training twice a week. Although only a small percentage of Libyan citizens actually get called to serve, they are ready.

The National Anthem

"Allahu Akbar" ("God Is Great!"), the title of Libya's national anthem, is also the Muslim call to prayer. The words and music were written as a battle song for the Egyptian army during the Suez War of 1956. When Muammar al-Qaddafi came to power in 1969, he adopted the song as Libya's national anthem.

God is great!
God is great!
He is above plots of the aggressors,
And he is the best helper of the oppressed.
With faith and with weapons I shall defend my country,
And the light of truth will shine in my hand.
Sing with me!
Sing with me!
God is great!
God is great!
God, God, God is great!
God is above the aggressors.

Human Rights in Libya

In 1988, the General People's Congress adopted the Great Green Charter of Human Rights. This document states that Libyan judges are independent, and that people have the right to freedom of thought. It also declares that men and women are equal, and that the government should not put people to death for their crimes. The government does not always follow these principles, however.

People must get government approval before holding public gatherings. Citizens do not have the right to form trade unions or political parties. The media are under strict government control—the government owns the country's daily newspaper and its radio and television stations. The government often censors foreign newspapers and magazines. The government also blocks some Internet sites.

In addition, it is alleged that Libyan officials use intimidation and terror to prevent people from expressing political views opposed to Qaddafi. Libya also has many political prisoners, and some are reportedly tortured.

Fathi Eljahmi is Libya's best-known critic of Qaddafi. Eljahmi has been locked in a windowless room without outside communication since 2004. His crime? He made negative remarks about Qaddafi to the international media. Earlier, Eljahmi was jailed for two years because he called for greater openness and freedom in the Libyan government.

The Next Leader of Libya?

Many people believe that Saif al-Islam al-Qaddafi, the second-oldest of Qaddafi's seven sons, will become the leader of Libya when his father steps down. Born in 1971, Saif graduated in 1993 from Tripoli's al-Fatah University with a degree in urban engineering. He later earned degrees from IMADEC University in Vienna, Austria, and the London School of Economics. He is president of the Qaddafi International Foundation for Charity Associations and helps represent Libya at international functions. He also manages an environmental group that teaches children what they can do to help clean up Libya.

The younger Qaddafi has hinted that he believes Libya should allow elections and more than one political party. "Democracy is the only way to improve our society because it is efficient," he said in a 2006 interview. "And it is efficient because it is competitive—the best person is chosen freely for the job. For this reason, democracy is critical to development. In much of the Arab world you are in government not because you are best, but because you are loyal to whoever is in power."

He has denied reports that he is preparing to take over Libya when his father relinquishes power. "Our country's political system should not be based on loyalty or lineage," he said during the same interview. "That would make a mockery of everything I've just said about democracy. We are not the kingdom of Libya."

Tripoli: Did You Know This?

Tripoli, Libya's capital, is sometimes called Tarablus al-Gharb, or West Tripoli, so that people can tell it apart from Tripoli, Lebanon. The Phoenicians founded the Libyan city in the seventh century B.C. Tripoli has been an important seaport ever since.

Today, Tripoli has an estimated 911,643 residents. It is Libya's economic center. Oil and other petroleum products leave on ships from its ports. Leather and carpets are manufactured in the city, which is also a base for commercial fishing.

Many Libyans enjoy the cooling breezes while walking along Tripoli's seaside promenade. Nearby are lovely beaches, good for relaxing and swimming. The city is home to Libya's national museum, the Jamahiriya Museum, and al-Fatah University. Tripoli's old quarter has a sixteenth-century Spanish castle (above), ancient mosques, and a marble arch from the second century.

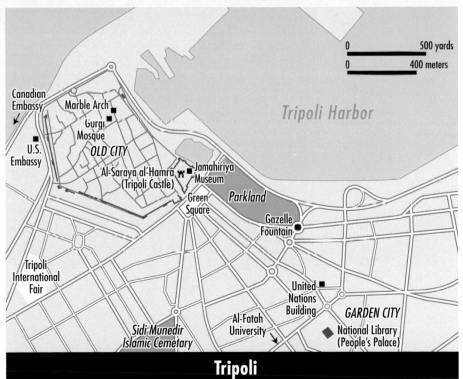

0   500 yards
0   400 meters

Tripoli Harbor

Canadian Embassy
Marble Arch
Gurgi Mosque
U.S. Embassy
OLD CITY
Al-Saraya al-Hamra (Tripoli Castle)
Jamahiriya Museum
Green Square
Parkland
Gazelle Fountain
Tripoli International Fair
United Nations Building
GARDEN CITY
Sidi Munedir Islamic Cemetary
Al-Fatah University
National Library (People's Palace)

Tripoli

The Oil Economy

L IBYA'S ECONOMY IS BASED SOLIDLY UPON THE OIL beneath the country's desert. Most of the money flowing into the country—95 percent of it—comes from oil.

Before the discovery of oil in 1959, Libya was one of the world's poorest nations. It depended upon aid from a number of countries, including the United States and Great Britain. Some Libyans had jobs in factories. But most people survived by farming or scouring the desert for food.

Opposite: **A camel wanders through a Libyan oil field.**

A Libyan oil-pumping station. Libya has more oil reserves than any other African nation.

The Oil Boom

With the discovery of oil, everything changed. Demand for Libya's crude oil was high. Libya's oil contains less sulfur than oil from other parts of the world, so it was easier and cheaper to process and cleaner to use. Foreign aid was no longer necessary to keep Libya moving. The country had plenty of money to spend on building roads, schools, and hospitals. The nation strengthened its military. Apartments were built for the poor. Thousands of jobs were created.

Many Libyans earned good wages working in the oil industry. They could afford to buy modern goods, such as kitchen appliances and television sets. As more people wanted these products, more people got jobs making them. More shops sprang up to sell the merchandise. Many workers in the oil industry wanted better homes, so the number of jobs in construction increased as well. The oil money improved all aspects of Libya's economy.

Today, about one-quarter of all the economic activity in Libya is related to oil. Libya is a member of OPEC, the Organization of Petroleum Exporting Countries. It has 39.1 billion barrels of crude oil reserves, more than any other African nation. Oil accounts for about 95 percent of Libya's exports. Libya sells most of its oil to Italy, Germany, and Spain. In recent years, many foreign companies have begun investing in Libya's oil industry. This has improved Libya's economy.

Other Industry

Libya also has an estimated 46.4 trillion cubic feet (1.3 trillion cubic m) in natural gas reserves, the fourth-largest supply in Africa. Salt and gypsum are also produced in Libya.

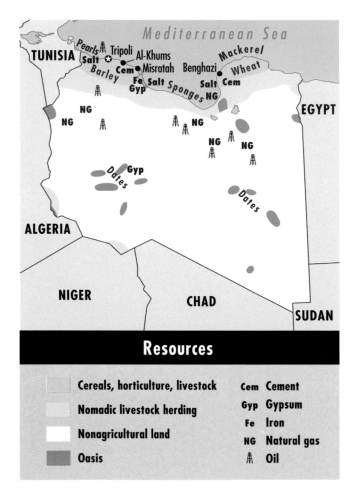

Resources

- Cereals, horticulture, livestock
- Nomadic livestock herding
- Nonagricultural land
- Oasis

- Cem Cement
- Gyp Gypsum
- Fe Iron
- NG Natural gas
- ⚒ Oil

Manufacturing and construction account for about one-fifth of Libya's economy. Refining oil is a major industry. Libya makes cement, chemicals, iron, steel, and aluminum. Food processing is an important industry. The nation also produces textiles and leather goods. Most manufacturing jobs cluster near cities along the coast.

Busy ports line the Libyan coast. Oil makes up the vast majority of the nation's exports.

Agriculture

Because most of Libya has poor soil and receives little rain, agriculture is limited. Libya buys about 75 percent of its food from other countries. Farms occupy only about 1 percent of the land. Another 8 percent serves as pasture for animals. Livestock raised in Libya includes chickens, sheep, goats, and cattle.

Most of the nation's farmland is along the Mediterranean coast. Cereals are the major crops, and barley is the most

common. Wheat and sorghum are also grown. Other important crops include olives, citrus fruits, apricots, figs, and tomatoes. Dates are the major crop in the southern oases.

What Libya Grows, Makes, and Mines

Agriculture (2000)

Wheat	160,000 metric tons
Barley	80,000 metric tons
Chickens	25 million birds

Manufacturing

Oil refining (2002)	11,531,000 metric tons
Cement (1997)	2,524,000 metric tons

Mining

Oil (2006)	1.8 million barrels a day
Natural gas (2005)	11.7 billion cubic meters

Many fish swim in the waters off the Libyan coast. But few Libyans work as fishers because there is little demand for fish in Libya. Instead, Italians, Greeks, Tunisians, and others catch the tuna, sardines, and red mullet found there.

The Souk

Many Libyans do their shopping at souks—lively, traditional markets where farmers sell produce and merchants sell spices, clothing, carpets, and more.

Souks are also filled with craftspeople, some of whom make their goods right in their stalls, selling such wares as jewelry, baskets, rugs, pottery, and leather goods.

Service Industries

Service industries such as banks, hospitals, schools, and stores make up about 20 percent of the Libyan economy. Until recently, the Libyan government held complete control of the nation's banks and other services, but that's changing. The government now allows private individuals and foreign countries to own such businesses. Foreign banks can now maintain branch offices in Libya.

Money Facts

The basic unit of currency in Libya is the dinar. Each dinar is divided into 1,000 dirhams. In 2008, 1 dinar equaled US$0.82, while US$1.00 equaled 1.23 dinars. Coins come in values of 50 and 100 dirhams and quarter and half dinars. There are also coins with values of 1, 5, 10, and 20 dirhams, but they are worth so little that people rarely use them. Paper money comes in values of quarter, half, 1, 5, 10, and 20 dinars. Some bills show images of important Libyan figures such as Muammar al-Qaddafi and Omar al-Mukhtar. Others show such typical Libyan scenes as a mosque, camels, wheat, and an oil refinery.

Many foreign laborers work at Libya's oil facilities. They come from countries ranging from Egypt to Poland to Vietnam.

Libyans on the Job

About 60 percent of Libyans with jobs work in service industries or in government. The others are almost evenly split between agriculture and industry. Unemployment is a major problem in Libya. Some experts estimate that 30 percent of the Libyan workforce are without jobs.

Libya's education system isn't turning out as many highly trained workers as the country needs to fill its technical jobs. As a result, many foreigners have moved to Libya to take these jobs. Many other immigrants have moved to Libya to work as manual laborers. About 165,000 foreigners live in Libya. They come from countries including Egypt, Turkey, and India.

Weights and Measures

Libya officially uses the metric system of weights and measures. This system includes such measures as the kilometer (1 is equal to 0.6 miles), the kilogram (2.2 pounds), and the liter (1.1 quarts). Libyans also use traditional Arab weights and measures, such as the *oke* (3 pounds, or 1.4 kg) and the *draa* (18 inches, or 46 cm).

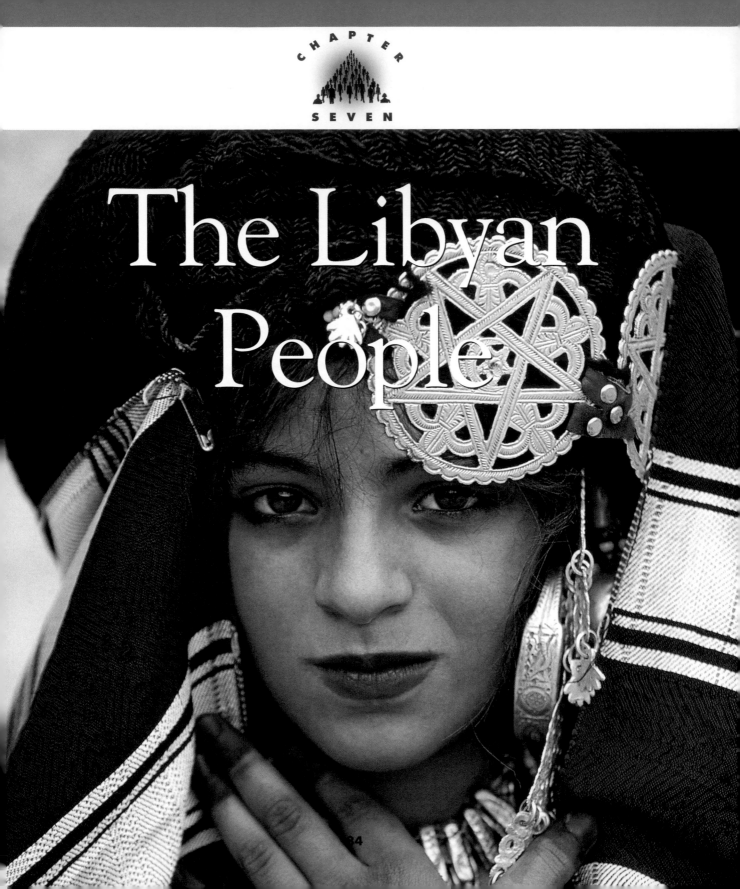

The Libyan People

ABOUT SIX MILLION PEOPLE LIVE IN LIBYA, ALMOST all of them in cities on the narrow strip of land along the coast. This is where the soil is most fertile; most able to provide the food they need.

Most Libyan citizens—more than 90 percent—are Arabic-speaking Sunni Muslims of mixed Arabic and Berber ancestry. The rest of the people include members of Tuareg ethnic group, Berbers, black Africans, and some people of Greek origin.

Approximately 165,000 foreigners also live in Libya. Many came to work in the oil fields or on the Great Man-Made River. People from more than one hundred nations live in Libya.

Opposite: **A young woman in traditional Berber dress**

Population of Libya's Largest Cities (2005 est.)

Tripoli	1,200,000
Benghazi	685,367
Misratah	354,823
Al-Khums	316,873

People from many different nations work in Libya. These laborers from Niger are traveling across the Sahara in hopes of finding work in Libya.

Who Lives in Libya?

Berbers and Arabs	97%
Others	3%

Nomadic Ancestors

The ancestors of most Libyans belonged to nomadic groups. Nomads moved from place to place, setting up camp wherever they could find resources. They were always on the lookout for grazing areas for their animals and food and water for themselves. Nothing came easily in the desert, but people lived this way in Libya's Sahara for thousands of years.

Some Libyans still follow this ancient way of life, but now it's mostly a part of the country's history. Some groups that once were nomads have settled in oases, and others have settled in small farming villages or in cities. Only a few nomadic groups remain. They include the Berbers, the Bedouin, and the Tuareg.

This image from 1824 shows Tuareg people traveling across the Sahara on camels.

The Berbers

The Berbers once inhabited most of North Africa. Today, they make up only about 3 percent of Libya's population, though most Libyans have some Berber ancestry. Berbers were not always nomadic. They once lived as farmers in small groups along the coast. As cities grew along the coast, the Berbers were pushed out. Most moved to the Jabal Nafusah highlands

near Tripoli, and many Berbers remain isolated in this area. In order to feed their goats and sheep, they live a partially nomadic life, sometimes herding the animals great distances to find water.

Most Berbers speak the Berber language but most are also fluent in Arabic. Although Berbers are generally Muslim, many have kept some of their ancient religious traditions. They honor their own saints and holy places.

The Berbers built this structure in Jabal Nafusah seven hundred years ago. The rooms were primarily used for storing grain.

The Bedouin have lived in what is now Libya for a thousand years. They migrated there from the Arabian Peninsula in southwestern Asia.

The Bedouin

The Bedouin are Arabs belonging to several nomadic groups who came to Libya in the eleventh century. The word *Bedouin* means "those who live in the desert." Some Bedouin are still nomadic herders. They travel with their horses and camels, carrying their tents and all their possessions with them. Other Bedouin have set up small farming communities near oases. These are the home bases for the young men who follow the herds in search of water.

Many Tuareg people wear distinctive blue clothing. Tuareg men cover their faces with veils. Many people believe that this is for protection from blowing sand, but wearing the veil is actually a social custom. The men often keep their faces uncovered while traveling but put on the veil in the presence of strangers and those of a different social class. Tuareg women do not wear veils.

Tuareg families live in portable tents made of leather. They raise livestock—mostly goats and sheep—and travel with their goods on camels. Camel milk is one of their main foods. Traditionally, the Tuareg were desert couriers, carrying goods across the sands from one region to another. Today, trucks and planes have taken over this service, and there are fewer truly nomadic Tuareg.

The Tuareg people live in the Sahara. Some live in south-western Libya, but more are in Niger, Algeria, Mali, and Burkina Faso.

About 87 percent of Libyans live in cities.

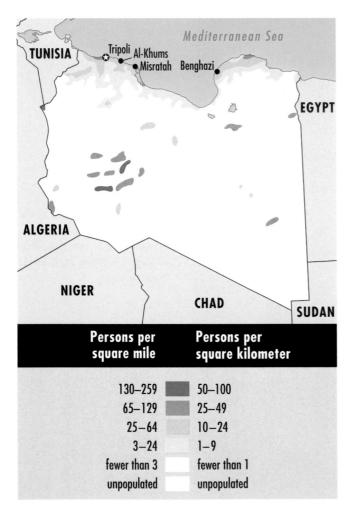

Mediterranean Sea

TUNISIA
Tripoli · Al-Khums
· Misratah   Benghazi ·

EGYPT

ALGERIA

NIGER

CHAD

SUDAN

Persons per square mile		Persons per square kilometer
130–259		50–100
65–129		25–49
25–64		10–24
3–24		1–9
fewer than 3		fewer than 1
unpopulated		unpopulated

A Move to the City

Most Libyans live in cities. Since the middle of the twentieth century, many Libyans have given up nomadic life, life in an oasis village, or farming, and moved to the city. The largest shift from rural areas to cities took place between the 1950s and the 1970s, following the economic boom that came with the discovery of oil.

After Muammar al-Qaddafi gained power, his government encouraged rural people to move to cities. It is easier for the government to provide services, such as education and health care, to citizens living close together. It is also easier to organize people into political groups, which is important to Qaddafi's *jamahiriya*, a republic in which everyone has a voice in government.

Today, more than 86 percent of Libyans live on about 10 percent of the land, the urban areas along the coast. Virtually no one lives in vast stretches of Libya. On average, only 8.5 people live in each square mile (3.3 per sq km) of Libya. Only seven other countries are more sparsely populated.

Many Libyans are young; one-third of the population is fourteen years old or younger. Only 4 percent are sixty-five or older. The life expectancy for Libyan women is seventy-nine years, while for men it is seventy-four years.

Libyan schoolchildren eating lunch. The birth rate is dropping quickly in Libya. In 1970, the average woman had 7.6 children. By 2005, the average woman had just 2.9 children.

The Arabic Language

Arabic is the official language of Libya, but English is sometimes used in government and business. Italian and French are also heard, as are a variety of dialects, or versions, of the Berber language.

Arabic also has different versions. Most Libyan children grow up speaking the Libyan dialect in their homes. As they grow older, they'll learn to read and write Modern Standard Arabic to communicate with others in the Arab world. In school, children learn classical Arabic, which they use to read the Qur'an. Libyans must learn different words and accents to be able to communicate in all these dialects.

Body Language

Libyans have a tradition of greeting strangers warmly. They welcome friends with handshakes and often embraces. But men do not shake hands with women unless women make the first move to do so. It's not considered proper for men to touch women other than their wives or sisters in public.

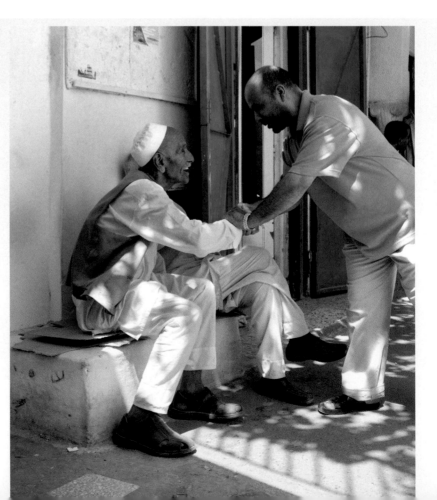

غسيل وتشحيم وتغيير زيوت
Washing Change oils cars

تغيير زيوت
Change oils

غسيل سيارات
Washing cars

تغيير أيطارات

A gas station on the road to Ghadames advertises its services in both Arabic and English.

Arabic is the fourth most widely spoken language on earth. It is spoken by perhaps four hundred million people around the globe, mainly in North Africa, the Middle East, and Asia. Arabic is written from right to left—the opposite of English—in graceful, flowing strokes.

Several words in the English language come from Arabic, including *algebra*, *artichoke*, *cotton*, *traffic*, *lemon*, *magazine*, *mattress*, *orange*, *satin*, *spinach*, and *syrup*.

Common Arabic Words and Phrases

aiwa or *naam*	yes
la	no
min fadlek	please
shukran	thank you
assalamu alakum	hello
bisalama	good-bye
ismah-lee	excuse me
Bikam?	How much?
Kam kilometric . . . ?	How far to . . . ?
Keef halek?	How are you?

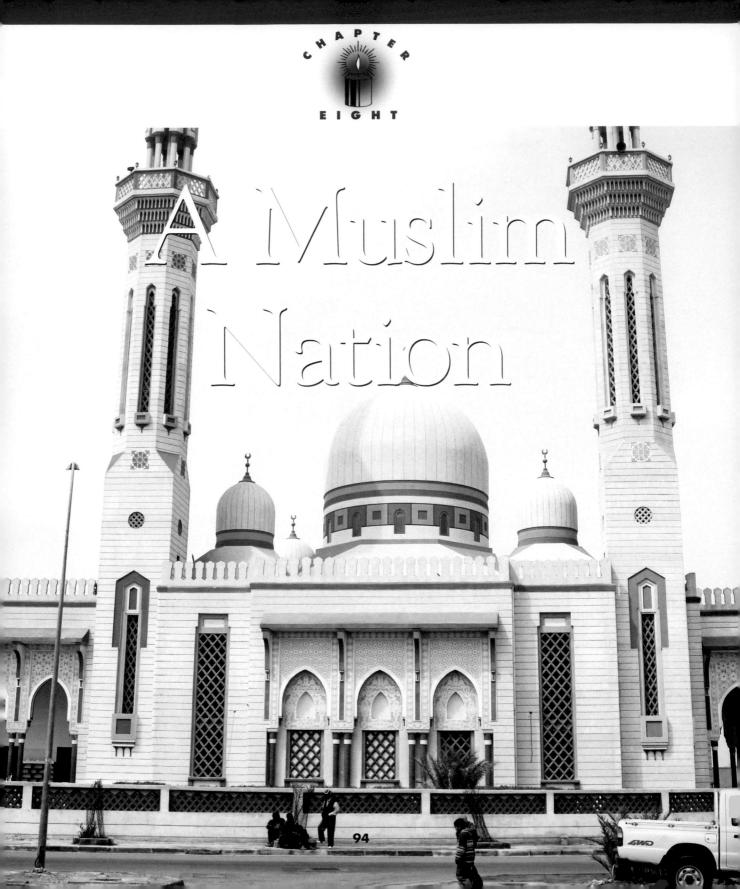

CHAPTER

EIGHT

A Muslim Nation

THE VAST MAJORITY OF PEOPLE IN LIBYA—ABOUT 97 percent—are Muslims, followers of Islam. The word *Islam* is Arabic for "peace, purity, and submission [to God]." *Muslim* means "one who submits."

Opposite: **A mosque in Ghadames. Most mosques include tall towers called minarets.**

The Origins of Islam

The story of Islam begins with the Prophet Muhammad. Muhammad was born in 570 in the city of Mecca, in what is now Saudi Arabia. Muslims believe that, beginning in about 610, Muhammad experienced frequent visits from the angel Gabriel. The angel brought Muhammad messages from God explaining how people should live, what they should believe, and how they should worship.

Muslims believe the Qur'an contains all the messages God sent Muhammad over a period of twenty-two years.

Muhammad began to share these messages. Eventually, they were written down in the Qur'an (sometimes spelled Koran). The Qur'an is Islam's holy book, which Muslims believe records the words of God.

Few people listened to Muhammad at first. His teachings angered the wealthy and powerful of Mecca. They particularly despised Muhammad's statement that God was the one great power, and that he ordered everyone to share riches with the poor. When Muhammad's life was threatened, he left Mecca. In the year 622, he began his journey north to Medina, also in today's Saudi Arabia.

This journey—the Hejira—gave Muhammad an opportunity to preach to people who were more open to his ideas. In Medina, many people accepted Islam. In 630, Muhammad and his followers returned to Mecca and reestablished it as a holy city.

This nineteenth-century engraving shows a mosque built in Medina in the time of Muhammad.

Muhammad died in 632, but Islam continued to spread. Traders carried their faith with them along with their goods. More important, Arab soldiers who were followers of Islam conquered other countries. The Arab soldiers—called Moors in North Africa—referred to their holy war as a *jihad*. Residents of the conquered lands became Muslims, too, and in less than one century, Muslim rule stretched from Spain in the west to Afghanistan in the east.

Mecca is the holiest city in Islam. Non-Muslims are not allowed to enter the city.

Islam Divides

Islam is divided into two main groups: Sunnis and Shi'is. These groups emerged in the years following Muhammad's death amid arguments over who should succeed him. Shi'is believe that the leader of Islam should be a direct descendant of Muhammad. Sunnis accept others. Today, almost all Muslims in Libya are Sunnis, but even in Libya, Islam has several factions.

Muslims always face in the direction of Mecca when they pray.

In 1837, a man named Sidi Muhammad ibn-Ali al-Sanusi began preaching to the Muslims of Libya. He started a group called the Sanusi Brotherhood and gained many followers. Sanusi stressed the need to return to the traditional teachings of the Qur'an and the fundamental beliefs of Muhammad. He sent teachers, called *sheikhs*, to live in the small communities scattered throughout Libya. The sheikhs instructed the people to build *zawiyas*, lodges that became central to the community. Each sheikh reigned as the community's absolute ruler. He was administrator, judge, and spiritual leader.

The teachings of the Sanusi Brotherhood were popular with nomadic Berbers. In parts of Fezzan and Cyrenaica, the Sanusi still have some influence. The Sanusi were powerful political leaders as well as spiritual leaders, and although Qaddafi has banned the brotherhood, memories of it linger with many older Libyans.

Another group, the *sharifs*, originated in Fezzan. Sharifs are people who claim to be direct descendants of Muhammad. Because of this, they are considered holy and supposedly possessed the power from God to see the future. Sharifs control many oases in western Libya.

Sufism is a form of Islam that focuses more on the mystical side of the religion than on the strict rules. It is personal and emotional, and its followers choose to live alone and without normal comforts. During the eighteenth and nineteenth centuries, Sufis formed brotherhoods, or associations, that were influential in Libya. These religious brotherhoods helped resist the efforts of missionaries to spread Christianity across Libya.

A Sufi mosque in Ghadames. Sufism dates back to the early days of Islam.

Muslim Beliefs

Muslims worship the same god that Christians and Jews worship. Many of the Qur'an's writings are similar to those found in the Old Testament of the Bible, and Islam respects all the prophets of Judaism, as well as the Christian prophet Jesus Christ. Muslims also believe in final judgment for humans: heaven and hell.

Marabouts

The term *marabout* was first used to mean a Muslim holy man. In North Africa, it later came to mean a Muslim missionary and then a Sufi leader. Marabouts are holy men who now live mostly in western Libya. They give up the comforts of normal society and own only the bare necessities of life. Though marabouts usually live alone as hermits, in a few rural regions they are accepted by the local residents and have settled in.

Marabouts often dance and spin wildly while chanting prayers in order to reach a trancelike state. They believe this brings them closer to God. Marabouts are said to have supernatural powers, called *baraka*. It is believed that a marabout's baraka remains in his tomb after death, so marabouts' tombs are considered spiritual places.

The hajj occurs over the course of one week during the twelfth month of the Islamic calendar. Each year, about two million pilgrims take part.

Rules for Muslim Life

Islam strongly influences the lives of most Libyans. Like Muslims everywhere, they follow five practices known as the Five Pillars of Islam.

One of these pillars encourages all Muslims who are physically and financially able to make a religious journey, or pilgrimage, to the holy city of Mecca during their lifetime. This pilgrimage, known as the *hajj*, occurs during the twelfth month of the Islamic calendar. In Mecca, pilgrims visit Islam's holiest shrine, a cube-shaped building called the Ka'aba.

A teacher watches while boys write verses from the Qur'an.

In addition to the Five Pillars of Islam, other principles guide the lives of Muslims. For instance, they do not drink alcohol or gamble. They do not eat pork or any other meat still containing blood. When lending money, they should not charge interest. They also try, in general, to be respectful toward all, treating others with honesty, generosity, and fairness.

The Five Pillars of Islam

The Five Pillars of Islam are rules that form the backbone of Islam.

1. *Shahada* is a statement of faith. Muslims must say, "There is no god but God, and Muhammad is his messenger."
2. *Salat* is prayer. Muslims pray five times a day—at dawn, noon, midafternoon, dusk, and after dark, facing Mecca each time.
3. *Zakat* is giving alms. Muslims should give generously to the poor.
4. *Sawm* is fasting, or going without food. Muslims fast during Ramadan, the ninth month of the Muslim calendar.
5. The *hajj* is a pilgrimage. If possible, Muslims make this special trip to Mecca.

Ramadan, the ninth month of the Islamic calendar, is a holy month for Muslims. They believe that Muhammad received the first of many revelations from God during this month. Muslims fast for the entire month of Ramadan, eating and drinking only before sunrise and after sundown. They believe that fasting improves a person's spiritual life. It cleanses the body and makes people more compassionate toward the poor.

Muslims celebrate the end of Ramadan with a three-day festival called 'Id al-Fitr. This is a happy time, when Muslims exchange gifts, buy new clothes, and enjoy delicious food and

Libyans crowd a market in Tripoli as they shop for *iftar*, the meal that breaks the fast each evening during Ramadan.

The Islamic Calendar

The Islamic calendar begins with the year of the Hejira, when Muhammad traveled from Mecca to Medina. So year 0 in the Islamic calendar is A.D. 622 in the Gregorian calendar, which is used in the Western world. The Islamic calendar is also eleven days shorter than the Gregorian calendar. Because of this, Muslim holidays fall on different days in the Gregorian calendar each year.

sweets with family and friends. They also remember the poor with charity.

Another important religious holiday is Moulid al-Nabawi, Muhammad's birthday. On this day, Muslims study the Prophet's words and life. In the evening, they celebrate with firecrackers, music, laughter, and delicious meals. 'Id al-Adha, the Feast of the Sacrifice, commemorates the willingness of Ibrahim (called Abraham in the Bible) to sacrifice his son for God. The festival coincides with the end of the pilgrimage to Mecca.

Muhammad's birthday is a legal holiday in Libya. It is a time of joyful celebration, music, and dance.

Both Tripoli (above) and Benghazi have Greek Orthodox churches.

Other Religions

When Muammar al-Qaddafi took over Libya, he reportedly began persecuting people who followed religions other than Islam. Qaddafi led a movement to force Jews out of Libya and to seize their property. Most Christian churches were closed, and one Roman Catholic church was turned into a mosque.

Qaddafi later softened his views on other religions. In 1976, Libya sponsored a Muslim-Christian discussion in Tripoli, during which he spoke of the need for greater understanding among Christians, Jews, and Muslims. But by then, most people of other faiths had left Libya. Today, less than 3 percent of Libya's residents are Christians and Jews. Most non-Muslims are non-Libyans who have come to Libya to work.

Arts and Sports

A shoemaker works in his shop in Ghadames.

Throughout much of their history, Libyans were isolated from the Western world. They were not exposed to much Western art and culture. That isolation helped them preserve their own rich traditions.

Libyan Art

If an artist is a person who creates beauty in the world, then there are many artists in Libya. Traditional arts are popular, and many skills have been handed down for generations. Leatherwork, metal engraving, weaving, jewelry making, pottery, and embroidery are all vital Libyan crafts. Craftspeople decorate everyday items such as blankets, dishes, and belts with traditional designs.

Opposite: **Libya has a long tradition of making glassware, metalwork, and other crafts.**

Art and Islam

Gold vases, intricate rugs, decoratively tooled leather goods—Libyan crafts-people create many fine pieces. But look closely. Something makes their work different from much of the artwork seen in the United States or Canada.

Following Muslim tradition, most Libyan artists do not depict humans or living creatures in their work. Allah and the Prophet Muhammad are never depicted in Islamic art. Muslims believe that it would be trespassing on Allah's role as the creator to make an image of a life-form. Instead, Islamic arts feature elaborate geometric patterns and designs. Such designs, called ara-besque, enliven many mosques and other buildings.

In recent years, Qaddafi expanded Libya's relationships with other countries around the world. Libyan artists have followed this lead. Modern art and fashion are becoming more popular in Libya, especially in cities such as Tripoli and Benghazi. Many contemporary artists incorporate traditional Libyan art into modern forms. Though the country has few art museums, the number of private art galleries is growing, providing up-and-coming Libyan artists with places to show their work.

Ali Omar Ermes is one of the most prominent Libyan artists. His large, dramatic works often focus on Arabic letter forms. Sometimes he adds poetic verses as commentary on social issues such as human rights, peace, and the environment. Ermes now lives in the United Kingdom.

The Jamahiriya Museum

The Jamahiriya Museum, Libya's national museum, is located in Tripoli. Artifacts from ancient times, when Romans and Greeks ruled Libya, are among the treasures on display there. The museum houses many pieces collected from Libya's World Heritage sites at Leptis Magna and Sabratha. The museum also displays items from recent history, such as the wooden gallows the Italians used to hang Omar al-Mukhtar, the Libyan resistance hero, in 1931. Also on display are the car Qaddafi drove in the 1960s—a light blue Volkswagen Beetle—and a bronze statue of Qaddafi riding a horse.

Like Libyan art, Libyan music is undergoing a transition, from traditional folk music to more modern styles. Musical instruments that have been used in Libya for centuries include the *oud*, a stringed instrument similar to a lute; the *darbuka*, a goblet-shaped drum; and the *al-nay*, a kind of bamboo pipe. Music is a part of almost all religious and social ceremonies and festivities in Libya. Rhythm is an important element, so many people clap their hands while others play drums and tambourines.

Tuareg women play a drum at a festival in Ghadames.

Songs often tell the stories of great triumphs in history or of difficult struggles ancestors faced long ago. Some traditional folk songs handed down by nomadic groups speak lovingly of desert sands or tell of journeys across the Sahara. People often dance to the folk songs, though women and men usually do not dance together.

Each year, Tuareg people gather for a festival in Ghat. It includes singing, dancing, swordplay, and camel races.

Many young Libyans perform Western-style music. Ayman al-Aatar won the 2004 edition of *Superstar*, the Arab version of *American Idol*.

Today, more musicians are blending traditional instruments and styles with modern music. Nasser Mizdawi, who was born in 1950, learned to play a variety of instruments at a music school in Tripoli. He became popular in the 1960s and 1970s while a member of the band Annusur. Today, he remains one of Libya's most popular musicians, blending Libyan and Western-style pop music.

Poetry is an important art form in Libya, and many Libyans memorize poems and recite them for others. Often, these poems have themes of love, religion, and patriotism. In the early 1900s, Seleimann al-Baruni, a resistance fighter during Italian rule, wrote the first book of Libyan poetry to be published. Through the years, Libyan literature inspired others to carry on the fight for independence. After Qaddafi took over, he made sure that published works of literature supported his government. Few works of Libyan literature have been translated into other languages, so only people who read Arabic have had the chance to enjoy them.

A bookstore employee sits in front of a large photo of Muammar al-Qaddafi. Many Libyan works of literature have political themes.

A Libyan player throws the ball in a team handball match against Egypt. In team handball, players try to throw the ball into the opposing team's net. They move down the court by passing or dribbling.

Sports

Sports are popular in Libya. Many Libyans enjoy water-skiing, diving, and swimming along the Mediterranean coast. Large Libyan cities have golf courses, bowling alleys, and tennis courts.

Soccer, known as football, is the country's most popular sport. Throughout Libya, children play football on organized teams in school and on the streets of large cities and small villages. Adults play on local teams, whose games draw avid fans. University and professional teams compete with teams from other Middle Eastern nations. Libya also has a national football team known as the Greens.

A Libyan boy shows off his soccer skills.

CHAPTER TEN

Daily Life

LIFE IN LIBYA IS CHANGING QUICKLY. NEW INFLUENCES are affecting the culture as the government opens up to the Western world.

Opposite: **Libyans shop at a market in Sirt.**

Education

All public education in Libya is free of charge, from elementary school through college. Libya requires all boys and girls to attend school for nine years, from ages six to fifteen. After that, they can continue with three years of high school or four

Libyan girls at a school in Surman in the northwest

years of vocational school. Those who finish high school can enroll in one of several universities. More than two hundred thousand students attend college in Libya. Another seventy thousand take classes at vocational schools.

More than 82 percent of all Libyans are literate, meaning they are able to read and write. This is the highest literacy rate in North Africa. Most Libyans who cannot read are older people who grew up in remote areas of the country.

At a school near Tripoli, some boys wear traditional clothes. Others wear Western-style clothes.

Revolution Day

Libya's most widely celebrated national holiday is Revolution Day, September 1. This is the anniversary of the Libyan Revolution in which Muammar al-Qaddafi overthrew King Idris. On Revolution Day, Libyans listen to speeches and enjoy colorful parades that fill streets throughout the country.

Wedding Traditions

Weddings in Libya are rich in tradition, though some traditions are now fading. In the past, most marriages were arranged—parents selected partners for their children. Today, most young Libyans choose their spouses themselves, though family approval is still important.

Weeklong Weddings

Traditional weddings in Libya can last a full week and are quite expensive. The first three days of the wedding celebration focus on the bride and her female relatives and friends. They gather in the bride's home to celebrate and to paint designs on her hands, feet, and dress using a mixture of henna and water. Bridesmaids also wear henna designs.

On the fourth night, the bride and groom receive gifts, and the next two nights are filled with singing, dancing, and eating, though male and female guests typically celebrate separately. The actual wedding ceremony takes place in the bride's home on the sixth night. On the seventh night, the bride joins the groom at his home, where she will then live. Wives keep their maiden names after marriage. It's considered an honor for young Libyans to have children as soon as possible after they are married. In the picture above, a Muslim leader is preparing a marriage contract.

Another fading tradition is the custom of men providing homes and large dowries—furnishings and gold—for their brides. With some 30 percent of the Libyan workforce unable to find jobs, many men don't have the money for a dowry. Also, because many Libyans have moved to urban areas in recent decades, there is a shortage of affordable housing for young couples. Marriage is becoming a lifestyle that young Libyan men simply can't afford.

The Libyan government is trying to help. Government-run charities provide the necessities for a dowry—even the oil for cooking rice to feed wedding guests. They also provide an apartment for the new couple. The government is trying to

A Libyan wedding celebration. Male and female guests celebrate the event separately.

build enough apartments so that, by 2009, it can provide one to every couple that wishes to get married.

The government also conducts mass weddings in different parts of the country several times a year. In 2006, two hundred couples married this way. These are far less expensive than traditional Libyan weddings. Many couples who don't join these group ceremonies have one-day wedding celebrations rather than the traditional weeklong festivities.

Women in Libya

Until the middle of the twentieth century, women in Libya couldn't vote and were frequently thought of as their husband's property. Since 1964, Libyan women have had the right to vote. Although women have the right to travel freely throughout the country, few do so unless accompanied by their husband or a male relative. Unmarried women are expected to live at home with their parents.

Traditionally, many Libyans got married in their teens. Today, some Libyan women are postponing marriage because their society still expects women to quit work after they marry. So Libyan women who want to complete their educations and enjoy professional careers sometimes choose to remain

Khadijah al-Jahmi: Pioneering Woman

Khadijah al-Jahmi was born in Benghazi in 1921. Her father encouraged her to get a good education, something few girls did at that time. In 1955, she became the first female radio news anchor in Libya. She went on to start popular magazines for women and children. Though al-Jahmi died in 1996, she is still revered by many Libyans for fighting to give women and children a voice in the culture of their country.

Libyan women have more opportunities than they once did. Many Libyan women now go to college and have professional jobs.

single. Today, almost as many Libyan women attend college as Libyan men. About 40 percent of urban women work outside the home. Many have professional careers working as doctors and teachers.

Libyan Fashion

Rabia Ben Bakraa is perhaps Libya's foremost fashion designer. She designed many colorful, flowing robes worn by Muammar al-Qaddafi. Through her fashion house Azyaa Karima, she also designs clothing for other Libyans. Ben Bakraa combines traditional Libyan styles with modern Western styles. For women, she creates gowns with bold patterns and intricate embroidered details. Her outfits sometimes include pants and long veils. Her designs for men's suits usually have a Western cut, but she embellishes them with embroidery and gold and silver threads.

Ben Bakraa was born in Libya in 1950. Her family owned several textile factories, hotels, and other buildings. She was attending school outside the country when Qaddafi came to power, and she remained in Europe working as a designer for many years. Her family lost most of its wealth when the Libyan government took control of their properties. At the time, Ben Bakraa could not return to Libya, but she missed the country and dreamed of going home. In the meantime, she tried to put a Libyan flourish into all the clothing she made.

Eventually, Ben Bakraa got to know Qaddafi's adult daughter, Aisha Qaddafi, who liked her fashions. Through this friendship, Ben Bakraa was able to return to Libya, where she began designing clothing for the Libyan leader.

Ben Bakraa hopes to distribute her fashions around the world. "We are a very refined people and have not been exposed extensively to mainstream culture," she says. "We are still fresh and have so much to offer."

Clothing

The Qur'an says that people should dress modestly, something that has been interpreted in many different ways. Traditionally, many Muslim women wear veils in public to cover their faces, and some also wear long, loose robes that cloak their clothing. Some women in Libya still follow this style of dress. These women remove their veils only in the parts of their homes where no men except close male relatives may enter.

This more traditional lifestyle is becoming a thing of the past. Most younger women no longer wear a veil. Instead, they wear colorful dresses or skirts with blouses.

Clothing has changed for men, too. At one time, it was common for Libyan men to wear long, flowing robes. Today, those are rarely seen in Libyan cities, although some desert dwellers still wear them. Most urban men have adopted Western styles such as business suits, T-shirts, and jeans. Others wear long, loose tunics and slacks with sandals.

Most young Libyan men, especially in cities, dress in Western-style clothing.

Dining Style

Lunch is the main meal in Libya. Breakfast and dinner are typically light. Meals are served on cloths spread on the floor or on low tables, while diners relax on cushions. Guests eat first, followed by the oldest family members. Libyans often eat by scooping up food with bread, though they also use silverware.

At one time, Libyans did little talking during meals, but that has begun to change since families no longer spend their entire days together. Mealtime now offers the chance to catch up on news. Traditionally, men and women ate separately, but this, too, is less common today.

A Flair for Flavor

Libyans love spicy foods. Many dishes have fiery seasonings. Bread is a staple of the Libyan diet, and pasta has been popular since the Italians controlled Libya. Many Libyans live near the coast, and they eat some seafood, but they do not typically eat fish. The Bedouin sometimes eat camel meat.

Couscous, a form of pasta that is more like rice than noodles, is served at many meals. It often comes with hot sauce and meat. Lamb is the most popular meat, but sometimes chicken and beef are served.

Couscous is an essential part of the Libyan diet. Here, it is mixed with lamb and onions.

Coffee, tea, and pastries are the perfect way to finish a Libyan meal.

Olives, figs, apricots, and oranges—and dishes that feature them—often round out meals. Other favorite fruits and vegetables in Libya include dates, grapes, watermelon, peas, potatoes, and onions. For dessert, Libyans enjoy such sweets as *baklawa*, a pastry with nuts and honey, and *magrud*, cookies stuffed with dates. Libyans drink lots of hot tea and thick, sweet coffee.

Facing the Future

Predicting Libya's future is difficult. Muammar al-Qaddafi is an unusually strong-willed ruler. Will his son follow him as leader? The price of oil sometimes fluctuates dramatically. Will it go up or down? And what will happen with the Great Man-Made River? Will it enable Libya to supply all its own food? When the water runs out, then what? Whatever happens to Libya in the future, one thing is certain: faith and family will continue to provide the framework and substance of Libyan lives.

Timeline

Libya History		World History	
People make rock art in what is now Libya.	ca. 8000 B.C.		
The Berbers settle in what is now Libya.	ca. 3000 B.C.		
		2500 B.C.	Egyptians build the pyramids and the Sphinx in Giza.
Phoenicians establish ports in Tripolitania.	1300 B.C.		
		563 B.C.	The Buddha is born in India.
Rome conquers northwestern Libya.	107 B.C		
Rome gains control of Tripolitania.	46 B.C.		
		A.D. 313	The Roman emperor Constantine legalizes Christianity.
The Vandals conquer Libya.	ca. A.D. 435		
		610	The Prophet Muhammad begins preaching a new religion called Islam.
The Arabs bring Islam to Libya.	643		
		1054	The Eastern (Orthodox) and Western (Roman Catholic) Churches break apart.
		1095	The Crusades begin.
		1215	King John seals the Magna Carta.
		1300s	The Renaissance begins in Italy.
		1347	The plague sweeps through Europe.
		1453	Ottoman Turks capture Constantinople, conquering the Byzantine Empire.
		1492	Columbus arrives in North America.
Spain gains control of Tripoli.	1510		
Ottoman Turks control Libya.	1551–1911	1500s	Reformers break away from the Catholic Church, and Protestantism is born.
		1776	The U.S. Declaration of Independence is signed.
		1789	The French Revolution begins.
The U.S. Navy defeats the Barbary pirates at Tripoli.	1805		
Sidi Muhammad ibn-Ali al-Sanusi establishes the Sanusi Brotherhood.	1837	1865	The American Civil War ends.
		1879	The first practical light bulb is invented.
Italy gains control of Libya.	1912	1914	World War I begins.
		1917	The Bolshevik Revolution brings communism to Russia.

Libya History

Resistance leader Omar al-Mukhtar is executed.	1931
Italy is defeated in World War II; Libya is freed from Italian rule.	1943
Libya becomes an independent nation, the Kingdom of Libya, under the rule of King Idris.	1951
Vast oil fields are discovered in Libya.	1959
Libyan army officers overthrow King Idris; Libya becomes the Libyan Arab Republic under the leadership of Muammar al-Qaddafi.	1969
Libya is renamed the Great Socialist People's Libyan Arab Jamahiriya.	1977
The United States imposes trade sanctions on Libya.	1982
Work begins on the Great Man-Made River.	1984
The United States bombs parts of Tripoli and Benghazi.	1986
Pan Am flight 103 blows up over Lockerbie, Scotland; Libyan terrorists are believed responsible.	1988
Two Libyans are charged with bombing Pan Am flight 103; Qaddafi refuses to turn over the Libyans for trial.	1991
In response, the UN bans air travel to and from Libya.	1992
The Libyan suspects in the Pan Am flight 103 bombing are turned over for trial.	1999
Libya says that it has weapons of mass destruction programs and that it will end them.	2003
The United States lifts most economic sanctions and ends its trade embargo.	2004
The United States removes Libya from its list of nations that support terrorism.	2006

World History

1929	A worldwide economic depression begins.
1939	World War II begins.
1945	World War II ends.
1957	The Vietnam War begins.
1969	Humans land on the Moon.
1975	The Vietnam War ends.
1989	The Berlin Wall is torn down as communism crumbles in Eastern Europe.
1991	The Soviet Union breaks into separate countries.
2001	Terrorists attack the World Trade Center in New York City and the Pentagon in Arlington, Virginia.

Fast Facts

Official name: Great Socialist People's Libyan Arab Jamahiriya

Capital: Tripoli

Official language: Arabic

Tripoli

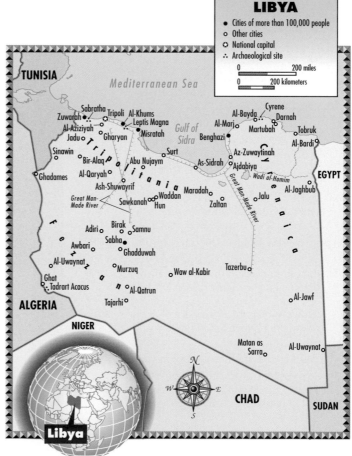

Libya's flag

Date palms

Official religion:	Islam
Year of founding:	1951, Kingdom of Libya; 1969, Libyan Arab Republic
National anthem:	"Allahu Akbar" ("God Is Great!")
Government:	Authoritarian state
Chief of state:	No formal office exists
Head of government:	Secretary of the General People's Committee
Area:	679,362 square miles (1,759,540 sq km)
Greatest distance north to south:	930 miles (1,500 km)
Greatest distance east to west:	1,050 miles (1,700 km)
Coordinates of geographic center:	25° N, 17° E
Land and water borders:	Mediterranean Sea to the north, Egypt to the east, Sudan to the southeast, Chad and Niger to the south, Algeria and Tunisia to the west
Highest elevation:	Bikku Bitti (Bette Peak), 7,438 feet (2,267 m) above sea level
Lowest elevation:	Sabkhat Ghuzayyil, 154 feet (47 m) below sea level
Highest average temperature:	88°F (31°C), at Sabha in July
Lowest average temperature:	47°F (8°C), in Tripoli in January

Leptis Magna

Highest annual precipitation:	16 inches (40 cm), near Tripoli
Lowest annual precipitation:	Less than 1 inch (2.5 cm), in the Sahara
National population (2006 est.):	5,900,754

Population of largest cities (2005 est.):

Tripoli	1,200,000
Benghazi	685,367
Misratah	354,823
Al-Khums	316,873

Famous landmarks:

▶ *Cyrene*, near Benghazi

▶ *Ghadames*, in the west

▶ *Leptis Magna*, near Tripoli

▶ *Marble Arch*, Tripoli

▶ *Sabratha*, near Tripoli

▶ *Tadrart Acacus*, near Ghat

▶ *Tripoli Castle*, Tripoli

Industry: The oil industry dominates the Libyan economy. The nation also produces natural gas and gypsum. Top manufacturing industries include oil production, iron and steel, cement, food processing, and textiles. The main crops grown in Libya are barley, wheat, and olives. Livestock includes chickens, sheep, and goats.

Currency: The dinar. In 2008, 1 dinar equaled US$0.82, while US$1 equaled 1.226 dinars.

Weights and measures: The metric system plus some Arab weights and measures

Currency

Schoolchildren

Muhammad Idris al-Sanusi

Literacy:	82%	
Common Arabic words and phrases:	*aiwa* or *naam*	yes
	la	no
	min fadlek	please
	shukran	thank you
	assalamu alakum	hello
	bisalama	good-bye
	ismah-lee	excuse me
	Bikam?	How much?
	Kam kilometric . . . ?	How far to . . . ?
	Keef halek?	How are you?
Famous Libyans:	Ali Omar Ermes *Artist*	(1945–)
	Khadijah al-Jahmi *Journalist*	(1921–1996)
	Omar al-Mukhtar *Resistance leader*	(1862–1931)
	Muammar al-Qaddafi *Political leader*	(1942–)
	Sidi Muhammad ibn Ali al-Sanusi *Religious leader*	(1787–1859)
	Muhammad Idris al-Sanusi *First king*	(1890–1983)
	Nasser Mizdawi *Musician*	(1950–)

To Find Out More

Books

▶ Di Piazza, Francesca. *Libya in Pictures*. Minneapolis: Lerner Publications, 2005.

▶ Ham, Anthony. *Libya*. Oakland, CA: Lonely Planet Publications, 2007.

▶ Hasday, Judy. *Libya*. Broomall, PA: Mason Crest Publishers, 2007.

▶ Miller, Debra A. *Libya*. San Diego: Lucent Books, 2005.

Web Sites

▶ **Arab.net: Libya**
www.arab.net/libya
For a good overview of Libya's geography, culture, and history.

▶ **Libyana**
www.libyana.org
A cultural site maintained by Libyan men and women. Includes information about art, crafts, poetry, music, people, and history, along with many links.

▶ **The World Factbook – Libya**
https://www.cia.gov/library/publications/the-world-factbook/geos/ly.html
For basic information on Libya's population, geography, economy, history, and more.

Embassies

▶ **Libyan Embassy**
2600 Virginia Avenue NW
Suite 705
Washington, DC 20037
202-944-9601
www.libyanbureau-dc.org/

▶ **Libyan Embassy in Canada**
91 Metcalfe Street
Suite 1000
Ottawa, Ontario, K1P 6K7
Canada
613-230-0683
www.libya-canada.org/index-eng.
html

Index

Page numbers in *italics* indicate illustrations.

Meet the Author

Terri Willis has written many books for young people, mostly dealing with geography or environmental issues. In addition to Libya, she has written several other books for the Enchantment of the World series, including *Lebanon, Venezuela, Qatar, Romania, Kuwait, Vietnam, Democratic Republic of the Congo,* and *Afghanistan.*

Libya has long fascinated her, especially the relationship between its longtime ruler, Muammar al-Qaddafi, and the nation itself. How has Qaddafi maintained his hold on the country since 1969? What are the benefits and the problems that have resulted from his leadership? And how have recent events around the globe affected Libya?

The search for answers began on the Internet. There are many good Web sites—and many bad ones. Willis points out that it's important to make sure any information taken from the Internet comes from a reliable source, such as a news organization or government agency, though even these aren't always credible. Embassies and recent books provided Willis

with further information. In the end, the picture of Libya that emerged was of a nation that has changed tremendously in recent years, but in some ways has not changed at all. Willis hopes that young people reading this book will gain a better understanding of how Libya remains dominated by Qaddafi yet is emerging as a cooperative player in world affairs.

Besides being a writer, Willis also works as an educator in elementary and middle schools. When she's writing a book and is not sure how to phrase something, she imagines how she'd explain the topic to one of the young people she knows. Willis has a degree in journalism from the University of Wisconsin–Madison. She lives in Cedarburg, Wisconsin, with her husband, Harold, and their daughters, Andrea and Liza.

Photo Credits